everyone agrees

BOOK I

words,

ideas, and

a universal morality

by J.S.B. MORSE

Everyone Agrees: Book I: Words, Ideas, and A Universal Morality.
Copyright © 2008 by Joseph Stephen Breese Morse. All Rights Reserved. Printed in the United States of America. No part of this book may be used or reproduced in any manner whatsoever without written consent by the author. Exceptions are granted for brief quotations within critical articles or reviews.

This book was produced by Amelior Publishing Company, an imprint of Code Publishing, PO Box 928483, San Diego, CA, 92192.
www.code-interactive.com/amelior

ISBN 1-60020-044-3

978-1-60020-044-1

*Dedicated to E.
for constantly clearing a path*

table of contents

author's note	v
introduction	1
apples and oranges	9
the greatest peak	13
the purpose	19
the game of life	22
part I: coca-cola, comedy, and confusion	27
in the beginning, there was the word	31
finding meaning	40
he's a bad man	42
who's who?	46
clear as a bell	50
define your terms	55
onward	60
part II: buddhism, bare breasts, and bureaucracy	63
believe it or not	66
the scientific god	70
keeping abreast on things	77
right, left, and down the drain	84
communication breakdown	92
onward	97
part III: science, socrates, and sense	101
relatively speaking	104
weird science	111
judgment day	113
it takes guts	117
everything i learned, i taught myself	121
he said, she said	127
onward	131

part IV: misdemeanors, machiavelli, and morality — 133

- slap happy — 136
- the golden age — 139
- the theory of concurrence applied to morality — 143
  - I. an act that is concurrent is innately right, and an act that is contradictory is innately wrong. — 145
  - II. a moral act can exist independently; an immoral act requires morality to exist. — 149
  - III. a moral act is good in and of itself; a right end does not justify wrong means. — 151
- lincoln's dilemma — 152
- onward — 156

part V: destruction, dna, and deliverance — 159

- napoleon dynamite — 164
- burn, baby, burn — 169
- life and death — 177
- let freedom reign — 186
- onward — 200

conclusion — 207

- notes — 215
- bibliography — 219

author's note

Just before the presidential election of 2008, I was awakened to a vile side of human nature. I don't make a habit of watching cable news programs, but, one day, I happened to come across a political commentary show that I could only assume was the norm for the television genre. The program showcased two speakers, each from a prestigious-sounding institute, and each in support of one of the two popular American political parties. During the brief time that I could stand to watch the verbal gladiator match that ensued, each speaker attempted to tear apart the other and denigrate the opposing party's presidential ticket.

The first speaker, focusing mainly on the Republican vice-presidential candidate Sarah Palin, launched into a rant in which he claimed that the Alaskan governor was unqualified, ignorant, and a horrible mother (presumably because she was running for office rather than helping her children with their homework). The opposing debater struck right back with claims that Democratic presidential candidate Barack Obama was an unqualified, communist egomaniac (the last modifier was no doubt fueled by Oprah's assertion that he was "the one").

When the conversation (if you can call it that) moved to the horrible claims each candidate's supporters were making about the opposition, the language became even worse. The Republican speaker protested that Democrats had called Palin's running mate, John McCain, mentally deranged as a result of his experiences as a prisoner of war. He also mentioned sick cartoons and videos that simulated violence against Palin. The Democratic debater then complained that the opposition had accused Obama of being a terrorist and had encouraged chants of "Kill him" at their own political rallies.

I was disgusted at the participants' lack of rationality and disregard to civility. I was also about to finish a book entitled *Everyone Agrees*, and it appeared that there was an obvious incongruity with philosophy espoused in the book and the behavior I witness on the cable news program. While I was attempting to show that, given the right perspective, everyone really does agree and all arguments can be overcome with rational effort, the display I had just watched indicated that the exact opposite was true—not only did everyone disagree in this political discussion, but they were vehement in their disagreement to the point of apparent hatred.

I took solace, however, in the principles I have explained throughout this book—namely, that disagreement only occurs because of the failure to communicate correctly or the unwillingness to do so. When people accept that there are some instances in which we simply disagree with one another, the claws come out and it's every political commentator for himself. The cable news program mentioned above didn't present two people who sought the truth while rationally disagreeing with each other; it showcased irrational name-calling and loud noises. The show's producers, as well as the viewers at home, seem to want that type of disagreement. But I've come to realize that yelling and fighting doesn't disprove the concept of universal agreement—on the contrary, it may prove it. To paraphrase G. K. Chesterton, people don't fight because they disagree, they fight because they agree that fighting is the right solution.

Hopefully this book will offer an alternative solution. The modern discourse between warring political factions, opposing religious practitioners, and everyone else sickens me, and I believe it's time to move in another direction. With *Everyone Agrees*, I have not attempted to push one political party on the reader; nor have I attempted to clarify which religion we should follow or what music we should listen to—that would be foolish and contrary to my real purpose. Rather, my goal was to show our disagreements are only fabricated and that we actually agree on much more than we appear to—even when it comes to touchy subjects like religion and politics.

I understand that the prospect of universal agreement is monumental and daunting. I'm reminded of this every time I mention the title *Everyone Agrees* and am met with immediate disagreement. "Everyone agrees, huh? I don't agree with that." But if everyone agrees that no one agrees, that at least shows that universal agreement is possible in some arenas. And if we can all agree that universal agreement is at least possible, perhaps we can make some progress in coming together for humanity's common goals. I'm optimistic about the possibility of universal agreement mainly because the ideas espoused here are reflected in much of the time-tested philosophy of past centuries, as well as in the works of the most prominent thinkers of today. To those thinkers, past and present, I owe a great deal of gratitude.

I'm also grateful for a remarkable support group of friends and family who all deserve my thanks. Most notably is my brother, Eric Robert Morse, who has helped dramatically in both the purpose and prose of this book. I probably wouldn't have started this endeavor without his influence, much less have brought it to a satisfactory level, and for that I'm grateful beyond words. I'm also indebted to my editor, Kristen Depken, whose amazing effort has enabled me to express the ideas in this book efficiently and effectively. A book about universal agreement wouldn't carry much weight if no one could understand it. For facilitating understanding, I thank you.

I'd also like to express gratitude for the social and technological climate that has allowed me to develop the ideas in this book and convey them to readers. Never before have humans shared such a wealth of knowledge, along with the ability to express that knowledge, as we do today. Unfortunately, there are mounting threats to the freedoms that have contributed to our current social climate, but, as we'll see throughout this book, there are also solutions to those threats. I'm hopeful that we can overcome the obstacles to progress and continue on the path to a greater life for all, and that the ideas in this book will contribute to that endeavor. With that sense of hope, I offer you the first book of *Everyone Agrees*.

J.S.B. Morse
San Diego

introduction

In October 2007, two highly contrasting ideologues met at King's College in New York to debate the value of the most popular religion on earth, Christianity. The premise was simple: one of the debaters was to provide an argument that opposed Christianity and the other was to argue in favor of the religion; the debaters fundamentally disagreed about the faith and were poised to prove each other wrong. The show lived up to its billing with fierce accusations flying and rhetorical jabs being thrown throughout. After each speaker fully laid out his argument, both remained ardently opposed to the other, but by the end of the forum they revealed something completely unexpected. What this dogmatic duo unwittingly showed the audience of attentive students—and the world—is that they actually agree.

The debate posed the question, "Is Christianity the Problem?"[1] and the two speakers were prime candidates to address the topic. Hitchens is a renowned atheist writer and scholar whose resume includes works on the *deist-not-theist* Thomas Jefferson, an irreverent criticism of Mother Theresa called *The Missionary Position*, and, most recently, the self-explanatory *God is Not Great*. D'Souza is a renowned Christian author and scholar who has written volumes glorifying religious America and the heavily theistic Ronald Reagan, as well as *What's So Great About Christianity*, the book that spurred the debate in question.

Over the course of the event, both debaters effectively argued their points, many of which were met with applause and laughter by rival collections of supporters in the King's College audience. On one hand, D'Souza thoughtfully explained the virtues of Christianity. It was Christianity, after all, which helped abolish slavery under the doctrine of equality in the eyes of God. D'Souza defended the plausibility of miracles on the premise that there is no scientific law to which an exception can't be made. He also countered the morality of atheism by pointing out the millions of horrific deaths that occurred throughout the twentieth century at the hands of atheist dictators like Adolf Hitler, Joseph Stalin, and Mao Tse-tung. To the open-minded viewer, all of these points helped to build a convincing argument in favor of Christianity.

On the other hand, however, Christopher Hitchens rationally explained the evils of Christianity. Scientific laws, said Hitchens, can't be whimsically suspended (as in the case of miracles), thus many of the tenets upon which Christianity is based are false. He noted the contradictory nature of the Bible, in which an omnipotent and merciful God also allows unspeakable horrors to occur. Additionally, Hitchens pointed out the dishonorable political ties that Christianity has held throughout the twentieth century (most notably the Vatican's connection to the Italian fascist Mussolini). All of these points made a convincing case for the atheist side as well.

I was personally convinced by the thoughtful arguments of both speakers. And as a result, I was also a bit confused; how could I agree with both debaters when their arguments seemed to be so contradictory? In essence, what is an open-minded and thoughtful viewer to think after witnessing a debate in which either debater produces rational and convincing points about religion or atheism—two polar opposites in philosophy? It seems like a paradox—Hitchens and D'Souza vehemently disagreed with each other, yet they were both right. How could this be?

For viewers of such a debate, there are two options: (1) one can pick a side with which to identify and ignore (or conveniently *overlook*) the logical evidence presented by the other side, or (2) one can scrap the goal of finding the truth and concede that there is no right or wrong in the first place.

The first option is the most popular in today's society, and it has a name: moral dualism. Most of the time, this mentality results in an "either/or" or an "us against them" proposition or question. Are you a Democrat or a Republican? Is it nature or nurture? Are you a dog person or a cat person? Was D'Souza right and Hitchens wrong or the other way around? Moral dualism, which pits one *team* against the other, provides many benefits to each *teammate*, including the feeling that one is a part of something and the gift of a goal in life, that goal being the desire to win or to defeat an opponent. However, such divisiveness stifles progress and usually ends in bitterness, betrayal, or some other ugly "B" word.

Despite its drawbacks, moral dualism is an extremely easy trap to fall into because of two factors: our cultural influence and our innate personal tendencies. First, we live in a society that promotes amoral competitiveness and thrives on divisiveness. From commentary by Rush Limbaugh and Al Franken to a sermon in church or an episode of your favorite sitcom, the *us-against-them* philosophy of moral dualism runs rampant throughout our culture.

An example of this type of philosophy occurs daily on talk shows like *The View*, in which women with different political and social views verbally scratch and claw at each other. In a May 2007 episode, co-hosts Rosie O'Donnell and Elisabeth Hasselbeck got into a daytime television rumble, the reverberations of which echoed for weeks and may ultimately have led to the end of O'Donnell's stint on the show several months later. Prior to this incident, the two hosts had already been positioned as left-wing conspiracy theorist O'Donnell versus right-wing Bush-apologist Hasselbeck. O'Donnell herself mocked the dichotomy, saying, "big, fat, lesbian, loud Rosie attacks innocent, pure, Christian Elisabeth."[2] In this particular instance, the two badgered each other on the proposed withdrawal date of U.S. military troops from Iraq and the legitimacy of the war in the first place. In the end, as is usually the case in heated partisan debates, nothing much was gained except further divisiveness and, of course, higher ratings.

Another example of moral dualism takes place every time politicians get together to debate. When John McCain and Barack Obama met for the second debate preceding the 2008 presidential election, they clashed on the true cause of the 2008 financial crisis. Speaking of the opposing Democratic party and Senator Obama, Senator McCain said, "But you know, they're the ones that, with the encouragement of Senator Obama and his cronies and his friends in Washington, that went out and made all these risky loans, gave them to people that could never afford to pay [them] back." Obama fired back by pigeonholing McCain as a "deregulator" and trying to put himself on the opposite side, saying, "A year ago, I went to Wall Street and said we've got to re-regulate, and nothing happened."[3] Each candidate blames the other side while positioning himself on the "good" side (with all of the nice viewers at home).

When someone attacks another person or group of people and forces them into an oppositional state, as is regularly the case on *The View* or in a political debate, the person on the attack is partaking in moral dualism, the philosophy that there are two mutually irreducible divisions in morality. Rosie and Elisabeth, Senators Obama and McCain, and Hitchens and D'Souza were all guilty of having the same dualist mindset.

While moral dualism may be easy to recognize on daytime talk shows and in political debates, it's more difficult to identify dualism from within, which is rooted in an innate sense of self-preservation and tends to perpetuate divisiveness even in the face of rational opposition. Once we identify ourselves with a particular group or ideology—such as a Muslim or a Democrat—we must defend that attachment or risk losing our self-identity. Neuroscientist Drew Westen gained insight into this phenomenon while studying the brains of political partisans during the 2004 election. He found that if we like a certain politician, our subconscious does some pretty hard work to maintain that liking. Westen showed that when Republicans and Democrats were shown contradictory statements made by their favorite candidates alongside similar statements made by the opposition's candidates, the partisans said *their* party's candidates were much more consistent—by a margin of two to one.[4]

Between the influences of our culture and the unavoidable

urges of our subconscious minds, it's no wonder we perpetuate the modern divisiveness so persistently, and it's easy to see why it's so difficult to change someone's mind. Convincing an opponent that you know what you're talking about and that he doesn't requires overcoming those cultural influences and innate human instincts, especially when the topic is important. As Harvard psychologist Howard Gardner wrote in his book *Changing Minds*, "It is never easy to bring about a change of mind; and it is even more difficult to replace a simple way of thinking about a matter with a more complex way."[5] Both D'Souza and Hitchens made intelligent and thoughtful points backing up their own positions about Christianity and religion, but neither was going to change the other's mind because each was stuck in the rut of moral dualism.

Those in today's culture who don't view the world as "us against them" will most likely adhere to another influential though less popular frame of mind: moral relativism. While the confrontational behavior of moral dualism is a problem for our society, it is not nearly as harmful as this alternative philosophy that is creeping its way into the zeitgeist. The basic concept of moral relativism is that we can't claim to know what is right or wrong because there *is* no absolute right or wrong (note: this is different from uncertainty—the moral relativist is actually certain that there is no right or wrong). The moral relativist usually avoids arguing altogether, but if pressed, will typically end a dispute with the plea to just agree to disagree. This approach theoretically promotes greater freedom of belief, but it also has the unfortunate side effect of being completely absurd. Lucky for me, but regrettable for moral relativists, I don't have to do much to disprove their philosophy because it ultimately refutes itself. If someone states that there is *no* right or wrong, they are really claiming that "I am right in saying that there is no right or wrong." But how can an *ideology* be right if *nothing* is right? Moral relativism, as an ideology, is the antithesis of rationality, the root of self-destruction, and the exact opposite of the truth.

To some, moral relativism may not be an ideology, per se; it may just be simple laziness that prompts some to agree to disagree. After all, who wants to argue incessantly about every little topic? But that laziness, if carried out to its ultimate natural end, promotes extremely destructive behavior. For example, if nothing is objectively *wrong*, then people should be allowed to do vicious and blatantly harmful things, like kick their dogs or treat women like chattel, because "that's just how they do it in their culture," and, "everyone's different."

In a debate, the open-minded, moral person is left in a quandary with only these two philosophies to choose from. Either he picks a side and ignores the validity of the opposing position (moral dualism) or he essentially gives up and claims that there is no right or wrong (moral relativism). Either way, it seems that an ultimate truth cannot be garnered from the discussion.

There is, however, a third way to perceive the debate on religion, or any debate for that matter; it's what I've termed the *theory of concurrence*. Simply put, the theory of concurrence says that which is concurrent (or consistent with itself) is innately good; that which is contradictory is innately bad. The implication of this theory, which I will elaborate on throughout this book, is that there is one ultimate truth and, given the same information, everyone really agrees on everything. I know, I know—it's a bold statement. But if you're open to some new ideas and some entertaining description (if I may say so myself), you may just agree with it by the end of the book.

Right off the bat, though, there's a problem staring us in the face. It's obvious that some people don't agree all the time. As a matter of fact, I could fill an entire book cover to cover with popular disagreements of the last few years (religion, politics, abortion, health care, the death penalty, taxes, global warming, the best NFL quarterback, etc.). Rosie and Elisabeth didn't agree on *The View*, Obama and McCain didn't agree in the 2008 presidential debate, and Hitchens and D'Souza didn't agree in their debate on Christianity. If everyone agrees, you may be thinking, they sure have a funny way of showing it!

The theory of concurrence answers this quandary. It states that if people seem to disagree, it's because they are miscommunicating in one of two ways: either they are applying two concepts to one word, or they are applying two words to one concept. When two people can't see eye to eye, it's not because one is blind; it's because they are looking in different directions. The theory of concurrence allows that we all have unique perspectives, but, rather than some being right and others wrong or there not being a right or wrong in the first place, we're actually *all* right but just limited in our understanding. Like loose individual pieces of a jigsaw puzzle, each perspective is part of the overarching concept. Only when they are locked into place can they be fully appreciated.

Hitchens and D'Souza fervently disagreed with each other, but it wasn't because one speaker was good and the other evil, as the moral dualist would have us believe. Nor was it because right and wrong don't exist and the truth is a useless notion, as the moral relativist would argue. The reason why Hitchens and D'Souza didn't agree is because they were talking about two different ideas. While both speakers appeared to be answering the question in the title of the debate—D'Souza explaining that Christianity was good for humanity and Hitchens explaining the contrary—in truth, D'Souza was talking about Christian theology, which has contributed to well-documented progress throughout humanity, and Hitchens was talking about the devious methods that have been used to control others in the name of Christianity. In this light, we can see that both speakers were right in their views, and both pointed to the ultimate truth of Christianity, but their *rightness* applied to different aspects of that truth; thus, there was no contradiction despite the seeming incongruity.

The theory of concurrence is a simple concept that helps to explain some very complex ideas, such as why we are destined to disagree on topics like religion yet can't help but agree on others like first-come-first-served seating. The theory of concurrence gives insight into why it's so frustrating when you can't convey an idea to someone and why that frustration can be so funny to bystanders who see the whole picture. In fact, the theory gives insight into why we laugh at all. The theory of concurrence also points to a completely rational and commonsense universal morality—a standard of behavior on which everyone can agree.

apples and oranges

If there is an ultimate truth in topics like religion, you may be wondering, how can two rational people like Hitchens and D'Souza be so vehemently opposed to each other? The answer lies in a problem inherent to human communication: one word can mean completely different things to different people. Though we may think we're talking about the same idea when we use the same word, we may actually be talking about vastly different concepts. Hitchens and D'Souza disagreed on *Christianity* because they were using one term to describe two distinct ideas and therein lies the problem. If the debaters had used one word to describe two different fruits, for example, we would recognize the problem as soon as Hitchens complained that the fruit was hard to peel and squirted juice all over the place and D'Souza appreciated the convenience and tidiness of the same fruit. The old adage that one can't compare apples to oranges rings true in this case, especially if just one word is used to represent both fruits.

When applied to the discussion of religion, we see that Hitchens and D'Souza were comparing apples to oranges and calling them both a banana. Hitchens' orange was a man-made organization used to control people, and D'Souza's apple was a divine philosophy used to free people. If translated to the debaters' personalized perspectives, the name of the debate may well have read "Is Freedom the Problem?" to D'Souza and "Is Fascism the Problem?" to Hitchens. This incoherence is obvious in the debaters' opening statements, in which the believer described Christianity as the root of morality, equality, and democracy, and the unbeliever applied the terms "celestial dictatorship," "persecution," and "child-hating cult" to the same term.

Had Hitchens defined Christianity in the same way as D'Souza, there would have been no debate. Each debater's goal was to associate Christianity with his own positive or negative ideas. But can one concept—in this case Christianity—really be defined by such vastly different ideas as the "root of morality" as well as a "child-hating cult?" If the theory of concurrence could speak, it would say "no;" each concept is distinct, but the innate problem with language confuses the two notions. This problem was acknowledged at one point during the debate when Hitchens actually noticed that he and D'Souza weren't speaking on the same topic. Hitchens criticized D'Souza for choosing "to attack a position I haven't actually espoused." Unbeknownst to Hitchens, both speakers were attacking positions the other hadn't espoused throughout the entire debate, not just in that one instance. No one would confuse the "root of morality" and a "child-hating cult," but replace those ideas with one word—Christianity—and confusion abounds.

The solution to this problem with communication is to simply define our terms. We can reduce the statement "Christianity is good" to a tautology so that it's either true or it isn't, but for two people to agree on the proposition they must first agree on the definitions of "Christianity" and "good." Hitchens and D'Souza obviously have different definitions for the word Christianity; Hitchens associates nasty, lying old men involved in a masochistic fairytale with the word, while D'Souza associates it with pure rationality and goodness. Thus, it is easy to see why the two would disagree on the statement "Christianity is good;" their definitions of "Christianity" were about as close as Hitchens was to becoming a monk.

For two people to have any sort of meaningful conversation at all, though, they must agree on *something*. As it turns out in a fascinating twist of the Hitchens/D'Souza story, the two opposing minds revealed that they actually agreed on one thing: the definition of "good." While making their cases about Christianity, D'Souza and Hitchens each showed that *his* position was the pathway to a universal good. That universal good—for both men—was liberty. D'Souza made the argument that Christianity paved the way for the abolition of slavery and established an environment that promoted the moral equality of men and women. Hitchens, on the other hand, praised atheism for its effect of freeing one's mind from a controlling and fear-mongering dictatorship. Without being aware of this connection, the opposing ideologues found common ground in the notion of liberty as the ultimate good.

The debate between Hitchens and D'Souza is a great example of three of the central concepts of this first book of *Everyone Agrees*: (1) if people appear to disagree, they are actually talking about two different things, (2) people actually agree on the fundamental concepts of humanity despite how they may appear to contrast each other, and (3) there is one universal morality that we are compelled to follow and which can be proven rationally. When Hitchens and D'Souza appeared to disagree, they were talking about different ideas, not the same concept. Ultimately, the two debaters actually did agree on what constitutes good in a human society—liberty—though one associated it with the label "Christianity" and the other with the label "atheism." As we'll see, this notion of liberty happens to be one of the central components of the absolute morality at the heart of the theory of concurrence.

These principles apply not just to the debate on religion, but to all of the debates of our time, from politics to the ever-so-divisive "who started it" argument that usually occurs between two siblings in the backseat of the family van. When people debate the existence of God, for instance, the discussion may become heated and result in hurt feelings and perhaps even violence. But the majority of debaters fail to define the term "God" in such a debate. As we'll see in Part I, most people argue about things for hours on end without first stipulating what it is they're arguing about.

On the other hand, some people argue about two different things but fail to realize that those things have more in common than not. For instance, a Democrat or a Republican may criticize aspects of the opposing party while ignoring the fact that both parties want the same thing—liberty and happiness for all. Their only difference is in the methods they plan to use to reach those goals. In Part II, I will elaborate on this point by describing how arguments arise from applying different labels to the same concept, and how we all really agree on the concept even if we don't agree on the label.

In Part III, we'll see how, after we clear up all of our miscommunications, there is common ground out there—something we can agree on. Evidence for a universal morality exists in science, in the Socratic method, and, of all places, in argument itself. In Part IV, I'll detail exactly what that universal morality is. In the final part, we'll see how the theory can be applied to some of the most controversial debates of our time, from the war in Iraq to the energy and financial crises. The theory of concurrence reveals that there is one logical rule we can follow to benefit everyone and our species as a whole; in short, something on which we can all agree.

the greatest peak

Rising up from the lush tropical foliage and jagged black rocks of the Big Island of Hawaii is an expansive volcanic mountain named Mauna Kea. The volcano is presently dormant, but before the geothermal machine was done inventing new land, it had created the tallest mountain on the planet measured from base to peak.[6] Though much of its 33,000 feet is under water, Mauna Kea surpasses Mount Everest's 29,000 feet by almost a mile. Mauna Kea is beautiful, awe-inspiring, and bizarre. And, as we'll soon see, it's also a perfect representation of the central concepts of this book.

An interesting aspect about the 300,000-year-old Mauna Kea is its climate. On the east side of the mountain is the rainiest city on Earth, Hilo; meanwhile, the west side receives less than fifteen inches of precipitation a year. Imagine a phone conversation about the same mountain between a Hiloan and a native of Puako: "Mauna Kea is getting drenched today," the Hiloan would say. "No, Mauna Kea is perfectly dry. I'm quite certain that's the sun shining down all over the mountain," the other would reply.

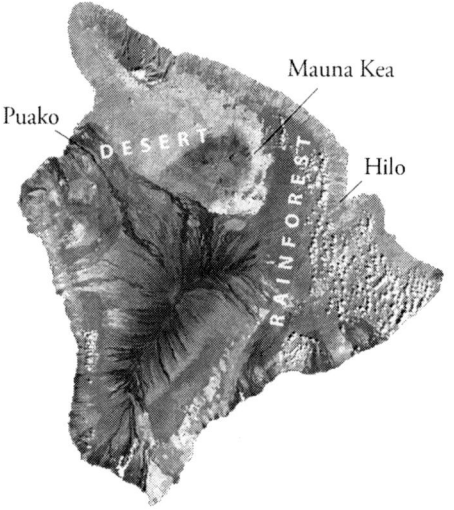

Fig. 1. People from different sides of the Big Island have very different perspectives of Mauna Kea. One sees the mountain as a desert, the other sees it as a rainforest. In reality, it's both.

Using the same word (Mauna Kea), both Hawaiians would think they were talking about the same place; but the two would actually be applying that one word to different concepts (i.e., the rain forest or the desert). In this way, Mauna Kea represents the first premise of *Everyone Agrees*: when people disagree, they are really talking about different concepts. "Mauna Kea" is one term, but when seen from different perspectives, that one term suggests two vastly different—even contradictory—ideas.

No matter which side of the mountain you're on, you can often see a cap of snow at its peak. Hundreds of years ago, the English-speaking missionaries to the islands would likely have called the imposing geographic structure something like "White Mountain" (Mauna Kea actually means "white mountain" in Hawaiian). And when they conversed with the native Hawaiians, disagreements would surely have arisen due to the difference in terminology ("Mauna Kea is sacred to you? That's okay, because we're only going to build on White Mountain."). Again, Mauna Kea serves as a perfect representation of the second premise of this book: people often use two different words to describe the same thing. In this case, English-speakers and Hawaiian-speakers may use different terms, but they're still talking about the same mountain.

These principles point to the problems inherent to communication, which are illustrated nicely in a quote by Albert Einstein. "Put your hand on a hot stove for a minute, and it seems like an hour," Einstein explained. "Sit with a pretty girl for an hour, and it seems like a minute. That's relativity!"[7] In essence, Einstein was pointing out that we don't always interpret reality the way it is; an hour is always objectively the same thing, but we conceive it differently based on our different circumstances.

Our thoughts are based on our senses, but they are not one in the same—as Einstein pointed out, they are relative to one another.

We have the ability to sense the world around us, then *make* sense of it and apply it to the past, the future, and other people. This distinctly human ability can be summed up in the dichotomy of perception and conception. All animals *perceive* the world around them, as do plants to some extent, but humans are the only species that can *conceive* of an idea. And ever since we've had the ability to think, we've used that ability to contemplate the difference between perception and conception. The dichotomy popped up in the ancient world in the guise of Platonic images and forms; it showed up in the debate between Enlightenment-era empiricists and rationalists; and the perception/conception duo also made an appearance in the famous works of Immanuel Kant as the terms *a posteriori* and *a priori* knowledge. The giants of philosophy have concluded that both perception and conception are integral to our humanness and both are required for our species' success.

The ability to perceive and conceive makes us humans special because it allows us to think, plan, imagine, and use the material provided by our universe to create something new. This great cognitive tool allows us to build cities, make epic films, and write books that describe things like perception and conception, to name just a few of its uses.

Unfortunately, this *-ception* duo is a bittersweet fruit that more often tastes like lemons than melons. Since our conceptions are independent of our perceptions, there is a likelihood that the two don't line up precisely, as seen in the Mauna Kea examples above. In the first example, the term "Mauna Kea" (the perception) did not line up with each native's description of it (the conception). In the second example, the natives had the same conception of the mountain, but their perceptions were different. Sometimes, the separation between perception and conception is beneficial. For instance, if we want to describe a play we saw, we can relay our *conception* of the play instead of having to reenact the entire event. Conception allows us to get the gist of an idea without being slowed down by unnecessary details. But that doesn't mean that if you ignore the details all will be fine and dandy. When we condense an elaborate perception or a series of perceptions into a summary conception, we can really screw it up (i.e., we can conceive of an event completely differently from how it really happened). And when we convey that conception to someone else, the chance for error in fidelity is inflated even more.

As we saw in the Hitchens/D'Souza debate, the incongruity between perception and conception can cause monumental rifts. When the debaters each perceived the word "Christianity," they conceived of completely different entities. Likewise, people may use two unique words (perceptions) when talking about the same concept. In both cases, the intended ideas are not conveyed, and confusion takes over. The result is disagreement.

This problem with communication is illustrated by an optical illusion developed by Swiss crystallographer Louis Albert Necker. Called the Necker Cube, it is a two-dimensional drawing of a three-dimensional cube. Depending on how it is conceived, however, the cube appears to be projecting to the bottom left *or* the top right. This works because the lines that make up the cube are intentionally ambiguous—they don't explicitly show which line goes in front of which. Thus, the same perception of eight lines can produce two different meanings or conceptions.

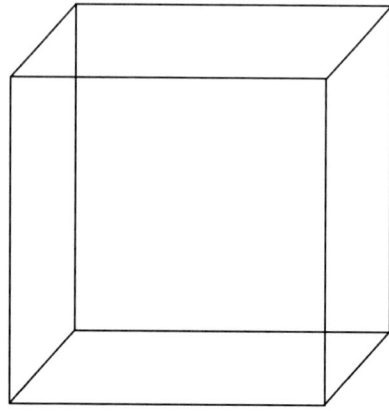

Fig. 2. The Necker Cube. The Necker Cube is a drawing that can be interpreted in two distinct but equally valid ways; the same illustration can seen to extend to the bottom left or the upper right.

If applied to the debate on Christianity, we can replace the two-dimensional drawing with the word "Christianity." The three-dimensional interpretation of a cube projecting to the bottom left would be Hitchens' interpretation, while the three-dimensional cube that projects to the upper right would be D'Souza's interpretation. We can easily see, then, how one word can imply two distinctly different concepts. All words are illusions; when these illusions are taken for the absolute truth, disagreements occur.

Just as the ambiguous Necker Cube can reflect any given word, the Hawaiian mountain Mauna Kea can represent many of the debates that go on nowadays. While Rosie and Elisabeth from *The View*, Obama and McCain from the presidential debates, and

Hitchens and D'Souza from the religious debate all have their rational perspectives of the mountain that is their subject matter, neither of their perspectives represent the entire mountain of truth. One of the participants in each debate sees only the rain forest; the other only sees the desert; and the idea of the entire mountain—the truth—is partially obscure. Thus, the third and final concept of this book represented by the towering volcano is that it is our goal as truth-seekers to ascend the metaphorical Mauna Kea in our debates and discussions—we need to see the mountain from both sides. When we do so, we attain the universal perspective on the subject and concurrence becomes a reality.

the purpose

My goal in writing *Everyone Agrees* is to uncover the objective of humanity, or what some would term a universal morality. To continue the Mauna Kea metaphor from above, we must rise above our individual perspectives of the mountain (it's a rain forest/it's a desert) and agree on a universal perspective (the mountain is both a rain forest and a desert).

But the objective of humanity, and likewise the goal of this book, is not to get people to agree on everything just for the sake of agreeing. The notion of universal agreement typically evokes images of forced consensus and totalitarianism that mean the loss of the individual and the obligatory adherence to the rules and ideas of a dark and menacing power. As the skeptic may claim, everyone in Nazi Germany agreed, but only after all the dissenters were exterminated. As an ardent anti-authoritarian, I can assure you that the goal of this book is not to *get* everyone to agree.

Rather, the goal is to point out that we already do, in fact, agree.

Since I'm a proponent of a universal morality, it may seem to some readers that I would reject diversity, but that's not the case. Diversity is good. It provides us with a colorful and vibrant world in which we can continuously learn and grow. As a contrast, just imagine a world in which everyone drove the same car, ate the same food, or knew the same people. Such a world would be unbearably boring—and no doubt a bit creepy in an Orwellian sort of way. Instead, we can drive the red sports car or the green Hummer, try the dish that we've never tried before, and talk to the good-looking stranger at the nearby table. We seek newness and diversity in our lives, and that's healthy.

But, contrary to popular belief, we don't seek novel experiences just because they're different; we drive the new car, order the new dish, and make new friends because we want to learn from the experience and possibly find a new favorite in the process. After all, if we don't try something new, we won't know what we're missing. Of course, we don't need to experience some things to know they're good or bad (for example, a Swedish massage or Chinese water torture), but without diversity, we wouldn't even know those things existed much less want to experience them. The point is that we don't do things to be different; we do things to learn and progress. Even the spiky-haired punk rocker, who claims that all he wants is to be different, still hangs out with a crowd of people who look exactly like him. In other words, diversity isn't the goal, even if people claim it to be.

Diversity is only good because it allows us to learn from new experiences. Imagine two ancient cultures that each used a distinct technique to plow farmland, one of which was far superior to the other. Suppose farmers from each culture met and exchanged their methods. The culture using the inferior method wouldn't continue to do so just for diversity's sake; it would adopt the better method in order to plow its land more effectively. Similarly, in the moral realm, two people who trade distinct ideas should not maintain both just for diversity's sake; rather, they should both adopt the superior concept if one clearly exists. This is the best path to progress and the most direct means of accessing the truth.

Just as diversity for its own sake shouldn't be the goal, agreement for agreement's sake shouldn't be either. Going along with the rest of the crowd for the sake of agreement isn't really agreeing—the parties involved aren't truly concurrent and usually end up developing animosity as a result of the pseudo-agreement that forces them to mask their true feelings. In this respect, agreeing just for the sake of agreeing (what psychologists call being passive) is no better than disagreeing. Even when people really do agree, the result isn't necessarily good. The Nazis all agreed on a lot of things, much of which was sickening and blatantly evil. Not all agreement is good.

When I say that everyone agrees, I don't mean to imply that we *should* all agree, and I certainly don't mean to say that we should all be *forced* to agree. That would, in fact, be counter to the central theory of this book. Rather, I intend to assert that we all already agree despite our preconceived notions and reservations about any given topic. You agree, too, though you may not know it yet.

Ultimately, the goal of humanity should be to ascend the metaphorical Mauna Kea and attain truth, and the goal of this book is to do the same. I hope to uncover important truths with regard to human nature and the nature of the universe, including the truth that we all have more in common with each other than we have previously realized. If we can uncover the goal of humanity, then perhaps a universal morality isn't too far off.

the game of life

One final point to touch on before *Everyone Agrees* gets under way is best illustrated by a completely made-up situation based on characters from NBC's *The Office*. In the sitcom, Dwight Schrute works at Dunder Mifflin as the Assistant Regional Manager or the Assistant *to* the Regional Manager (depending on who you ask). Dunder Mifflin has a strict policy on when employees must clock in and out, but Dwight has Goju-Ryu karate classes and volunteer sheriff duties in the morning, which often make him late to work. His supervisor, Michael Scott, is not a happy camper when Dwight is late, and Michael has reprimanded Dwight for "trying to thwart his authority." The more Dwight is reprimanded, the more he wants to release what he refers to as his "secret evidence," which Dwight claims will bring Michael down and allow Dwight to take his position as Regional Manager. Dwight's comical quirks aside, this example reflects conflicts common to today's workplace, and it can be used to demonstrate how we can employ the theory of concurrence in our daily lives.

Dwight and Michael are both compelled to continue their feud. Even though Dwight loves his work, he absolutely must fulfill his karate and sheriff duties. Meanwhile, Michael, though he wants friends more than he wants obedient employees, must show that he is in control of his underlings. The two are both right in their sentiments; as a result, they seem to be at an impasse.

However, the two have the option to resolve their conflict, and that's just what Dwight does.

For an entire week, Dwight counts the number of positive sales responses he receives in the hour after his normal starting time of eight a.m. and in the hour after his normal quitting time of five p.m. Dwight discovers that there are more sales in the five to six time slot than in the morning, and he sees a potential solution.

Dwight presents his finding to Michael and requests that he change his shift to nine to six in order to fulfill his morning obligations and benefit the company by working during the more lucrative sales period. Dwight wanted what was best for himself, but, instead of pitting the Assistant against the Regional Manager by coming in late, he created a solution that helped everyone involved. Instead of continuing a win-lose conflict, he invented a win-win situation.

Economists use a tool called game theory to help understand situations like these. In game theory, complex social behavior is whittled down to specific decisions in the form of a game. When people think of games, football, tennis, and perhaps chess and checkers come to mind. Economists utilize simpler games like rock-paper-scissors and matching pennies, but all of these, from football to chess, are zero-sum games in which there is only one winner and one loser, regardless of whether the game is played by one person or a team. Though these games are entertaining to watch and to play, they are distinctly unlike reality in one substantial way: life is a non-zero-sum game in that it has the potential for both win-win and lose-lose situations.

But economists, wily as they are, have also devised games that emulate the complexities of the non-zero-sum reality. An example of a non-zero-sum game is one in which two drivers are driving cars toward each other at high speeds. At the last moment, the participants must decide which way to steer their cars. If both drivers pick the same direction—choosing to swerve to the right, for instance—both drivers will be able to drive on, and both will win. On the other hand, if the drivers pick different directions and one swerves left as the other swerves right, they will both end up with an airbag in the face and a higher insurance bill.

In this driving game, it's easy to see the value of coordinating, and, for the most part, drivers in the real world choose to coordinate so that everyone benefits. But in complex social situations—as in the Dwight/Michael case above—coordination is not an obvious panacea. Not only did Dwight and Michael have to consider Dwight's hours, they each had to factor in the other's personal feelings. Both comic characters could have seen the situation as a "me-against-him" battle in which there could only be one winner and one loser, but this mentality only creates an unpleasant workplace.

Like Dwight and Michael, we are given a choice in each of our own conflicts and disagreements. We can look at the world as a zero-sum game in which our individual perspectives dominate the public forum, or we can aim for a universal perspective and realize that there is the potential for everyone to win. We can continue to view the world as "us against them," Republican versus Democrat, atheist versus believer, or we can choose to work together. Only one of these options will allow humanity to continue to exist on its current scale. Bill Clinton, one of the most divisive U.S. presidents of our time, described this point succinctly in an interview with *Wired* magazine:

> *The more complex societies get and the more complex the networks of interdependence within and beyond community and national borders get, the more people are forced in their own interests to find non-zero-sum solutions. That is, win–win solutions instead of win–lose solutions . . . Because we find as our interdependence increases that, on the whole, we do better when other people do better as well—so we have to find ways that we can all win.*[8]

The validity of this quote should resonate no matter which side of the political aisle you reside on.

My hope is that this book will provide helpful insight into how best to coordinate with each other in the game of life—to attain a universal perspective, in other words. Once we do that we can move beyond our divisive past. As another polarizing U.S. president, George W. Bush, once said, "I think we agree, the past is over."[9] With any luck, we will all be able to agree on the future as well.

part I

coca-cola, comedy, and confusion

When the soft drink behemoth and branding superpower Coca-Cola decided to open up its market to a fifth of the world's population in China near the end of the 1920s, a problem arose. The Coke execs wanted to maintain the pronunciation of the brand so that customers would ask for a "Coca-Cola" just as they do in English-speaking countries. But when Chinese shopkeepers created their own signs to promote the beverage, putting together a string of Mandarin characters that were pronounced "ko-ka-ko-la," the characters they used meant something completely incomprehensible. Instead of promoting Coca-Cola, they really advertised what translated to "female horse fastened with wax," "wax-flattened mare," or, my favorite, "bite the wax tadpole." I don't know about you, but nothing sounds more refreshing to me than a tall glass of "bite the wax tadpole!"[1]

Those names certainly wouldn't do, so Coke execs sorted through 40,000 Mandarin characters—two hundred of which were suitable for the sounds they were trying to produce. Still, nothing quite represented a beverage one would want to drink. So they compromised and chose "lé" instead of the troublesome "la" sound to create the genius **可口可樂**. The new phrase sounded like "Coca-Cola" and meant "to allow the mouth to be able to rejoice." One can imagine how sales were affected when stores began marketing "happy taste buds" instead of a "wax-flattened mare."

This story shows how Coke marketing execs overcame the language barrier between English and Chinese and got everyone on the same page—if only for the sake of selling a few million bottles of brown carbonated liquid. While urban legend tells a different story, claiming egocentric Coca-Cola marketers pushed the nonsensical phrases above (instead of the Chinese shopkeepers who were actually responsible), the execs did in fact realize that the word "Coca-Cola" didn't quite convey the same idea in Chinese, so they took great pains to find a suitable alternative and make sure their meaning wasn't being confused.

The Coke marketing genius seems to be one of a kind, but most of us fail to realize that situations similar to the Coke problem arise in our lives every day, even without the obvious language barrier. Communicating our ideas effectively and efficiently is a task that is as difficult as it is underappreciated. Finnish Communications Professor Osmo Wiio once summed up this notion in a Murphy's Law-esque manner by saying, "Communication usually fails, except by accident."[2] And it's no wonder; just look at the complexity of communication. An idea is developed in one person's mind, translated into some form of communication (speech, writing, text-messaging), perceived by another person (usually with some loss in fidelity), and finally translated into an idea in the second person's mind. One of the main problems we face in communication is that since we all use the same words, we assume that they have the same definitions. People think they're on the same page when they are actually in completely different books. This form of miscommunication happens in all types of situations: in arguments about the quality of music, in political discussions, and, as we saw in the introduction, in religious debates.

Hitchens and D'Souza—both of whom confused words with their meanings—are just two figures in the vast debate about religion. On one side of the broader discussion there is Hitchens, biologist Richard Dawkins, philosopher Daniel Dennett, and the fifteen percent of the world's population who claim that religion is "violent, irrational, intolerant, allied to racism and tribalism and bigotry, invested in ignorance and hostile to free inquiry, contemptuous of women and coercive toward children."[3] Or something along those lines. On the other side of the debate stand D'Souza, biologist Francis Collins, spiritual teacher Deepak Chopra, and the other eighty-five percent of humanity who think that religion is a pretty darned good idea, including 2.1 billion Christians, 1.5 billion Muslims, and nearly one billion Hindus.

On each side of this debate are groups of clever, thoughtful, and recognized intellectuals who have found themselves diametrically opposed to each other on a topic that has been around since well before people knew what "diametrically" meant. How can this be possible? How can a collection of extremely competent minds have such vastly different views on the same exact thing? How can some rational people see a single institution as the scourge of humanity, while others see the same institution as the direct opposite, the savior of mankind? Could it be that the two groups aren't talking about the same thing?

The concept that I will attempt to advance in this part of the book answers that exact question in the affirmative. When two people or two groups appear to disagree, they are really talking about two different things, or at least two different aspects of the same thing. They use the same labels, but those words have markedly different connotations to the individual participants in the debate. Just as "ko-ka-ko-la" meant a refreshing drink to an American and a wax-flattened mare to a Chinese consumer, "religion" implies something different to atheists than it does to religious adherents. Religion, to Hitchens, Dawkins, and Dennett, is a manmade organization designed to coerce people into doing things for the benefit of a few leaders. To D'Souza, Chopra, and Collins, however, religion is a vehicle used to uncover truth, give people hope and happiness, and promote morality. Each participant's definition comes from his respective research, analysis of the subject, and personal experience, all of which is unique to each person. The reason why the two groups perceive the term "religion" so differently isn't because the group representing one side of the debate has been fooled while the group representing the other is a bunch of geniuses. Nor is it because there is no absolute truth to what religion is. Rather, it's because "religion" is one word being applied to two distinct concepts.

Disagreement is nothing more than a lack of clarity, and once clarity is attained, it's easy to see that everyone really agrees. We will see that both sides of the religious argument, and in fact most public debates and interpersonal arguments, hold valid and rational points of view. Though they seem to disagree, this is simply because they are not communicating their ideas effectively. This is an easy trap to fall into because of a subtle but extremely problematic aspect of human communication: we confuse the labels we hear in conversations with the ideas we have in our heads. In essence, we blur the relationship between perceptions and conceptions and assume that everyone shares our single perspective. Our ability to translate ideas and concepts into communicative language is our most effective and efficient way means of transmitting ideas; but with language comes the potential for miscommunication, which is detrimental to society if it goes unrecognized.

However, if we can reconcile two rational yet seemingly oppositional mindsets—the sure ingredients for an argument—we will find that everyone actually agrees. As it turns out, the same processes that help us reconcile our disagreements also allow us to live more entertaining and enlightening lives. As we'll see, the brain processes involved in sorting out disagreements are the same processes that make us laugh and enable us to make scientific discoveries. So, sit back with a tall glass of **可口可樂** and enjoy the first part of *Everyone Agrees*.

in the beginning, there was the word

The intellectual war over the validity of religion has been intensifying recently, as heated debates between thinkers spur the sensationalist comments of media pundits and acts of violence by militants. But amidst all the uproar over God and the existence of such a being, the participants have forgotten one integral aspect of the debate on God: the definition of "God." In fact, both religious believers and atheists forgot to define many concepts pertinent to their debate—including religion itself. The result is endless argumentative toil and tumult. In this section, I'll attempt to dissect the different opinions held by atheists and believers, and, with a little explanation, I'll show that even these two so seemingly opposed groups actually agree, and that what seems to be a disagreement is actually a case of defining the same words in different ways.

To be consistent with my thesis, I'd like to start by actually defining the labels given to each party involved in the debate about God. A believer is someone who puts faith in God, whether it's the supernatural, personal being that many Christians believe in or the detached, impersonal God of Einstein. An atheist is someone who does not believe a god exists, whether it is the unmoved mover of Aristotle or the unknowable but kingly God of Islam. While many people associate morality with belief in God, I recognize a clear dissociation. A believer in God can act immorally and, conversely, an atheist can act morally. Sure, a person's core belief system will impact his or her actions, but, on the surface at least, morality is independent of belief in God.

The differences in definitions persist throughout the division between believers and atheists. For instance, ask an atheist what religion represents and he will naturally categorize religion as a form of coercion since he thinks that the central component of religion—God—doesn't exist. Ask a believer what religion represents, and he will tell you the complete opposite—that coercion and its uglier manifestations in the form of oppression, slavery, and war are in direct opposition to the foundations of organized religion. Moses was the voice of liberty, not totalitarianism, when he told Pharaoh, "Let my people go." Ask a Christian what the Bible is, and he'll claim that it's an historical text that describes the truth about a miraculous man. Ask an atheist the same question, and he'll tell you that the Bible is an ancient poem about demons and fairies. Ask an atheist what an Islamic imam or a Jewish rabbi is, and the reply will be "a charlatan;" ask a believer in those faiths the same question, and the answer will be "a speaker of truth."

As you may have concluded, atheists and believers have different definitions for the terms "religion," "the Bible," "imam," and "rabbi." It makes sense then that when an atheist and a believer get together to discuss these ideas, they will find it difficult to agree. The reason for this: if there is a disconnect between the way two people define the same words, those two people will surely disagree.

Imagine a hypothetical scene in *The Office* in which manager Michael Scott, who is constantly trying to stay relevant, seeks the latest slang word in an effort to sound cool. After irreverently asking warehouse manager Darryl whether he's ever been in a gang, Michael asks what words the gang members use to mean "hip." Darryl, with a believable face says, "Michael, you need to tell people that you're a *tool*. It's what all the gang members use to compliment themselves. It means you're the man."

Michael begins using the word immediately, but he can't understand why everyone laughs at him when he makes claims like, "I know I'm the coolest darn tool in Scranton." After all, Darryl lied and misinformed Michael—"tool" actually means "dork." When Michael interrupts a group of obviously slang-savvy employees, he blurts out, "Hey homies, can this tool join the tool shed?" The answer would most certainly be "no."

This simple misunderstanding represents the central problem

with communication today: people have different definitions for one word but assume they are referring to the same thing. This problem is also showcased in the argument between believers and atheists. While Michael and his employees had different definitions for the word "tool," atheists and believers disagree on the definition of the concise but heavily loaded word "God."

This tough problem seems to have an easy fix: if you want to come to an agreement, just ask for a definition. But rarely do people bother to slow down a feisty argument in order to see whether they really do disagree with the other party. Unlike many of the participants in the debate over God, however, I did want to find out how believers and atheists defined the word "God," as well as what characteristics they attributed to the concept. So I asked them.

Over a period of six months, I asked participants (people who claimed to believe in God and people who claimed to be atheists) to describe their impression of God via two online polls[4]—one which allowed respondents to define the controversial celestial presence in their own words and one which required respondents to select their definitions from a designated list of words. For believers, this was a fairly straightforward task, as those who believe in something usually have a clear idea about the characteristics of that something. For atheists, the task was a bit different. Since they don't believe God exists, some found it difficult to describe the concept. "How can I describe something that doesn't exist?" they protested.

Their point was well taken, but also easy to resolve. I certainly don't think the Easter Bunny exists, but I can tell you a few things about it: it's around five feet tall and wears a lot of really tacky pastel-colored garments. As humans, we may be restricted by egocentricities and physical flaws, but we certainly aren't restricted by our lack of imagination; thus, describing something that doesn't exist should be a feasible task. Likewise, if someone doesn't know with what characteristics to describe something, how can he or she be certain of another characteristic for that something, specifically its existence? The only reason I know that the Easter Bunny doesn't exist is because I know that five-foot tall rabbits don't exist; even if they did, they surely wouldn't wear tacky pastel-colored garments. My goal in this poll was to determine how atheists, who assert that God does not exist, define that God, and to compare their definitions to those of the believers who assert that God does exist. The results were often humorous and thoroughly enlightening.

Love. This is the word that believers used most often to describe God. In fact, almost 75 percent of believers polled said that God is love (or loving), a characteristic that is becoming much more synonymous with the deity every day. Some respondents were more explanatory, quoting the passage from the Bible in which John writes, "Whoever does not love does not know God, because God is love."

Other popular characteristics attached to the believers' concept of God include (in order of popularity) "just," "merciful," and "graceful"—all very positive traits. Believers also see God as "kind," "forgiving," and "benevolent." Some took a humorous approach and characterized God as having "happy bugs flying around his head."

I'm no psychologist, but since they believe such a positive entity exists, I'd guess that these respondents must be extremely optimistic people. In essence, they believe that love, justice, and mercy exist, and that those qualities are embodied in a being they call "God."

On the other side of the equation, those respondents who claimed to be atheists had a much different take on the concept of God. Apart from taking a more frivolous approach to the poll (Morgan Freeman was mentioned a number of times as the embodiment of God, no doubt because of his *godly* acting in movies like *Bruce Almighty*), atheists seemed to have a distinctly negative concept of God in their heads. With the atheists, one word represented God more universally than any other: "nothing." 32.5 percent of the atheist respondents used this word to label the nonexistent God. But besides that tautological reference, atheists saw God as "selfish," "hateful," "unjust," "vengeful," "controlling," and "contradictory" (in order of popularity). If I thought a particular being was associated with those words, I would hope it didn't exist, too, and I certainly wouldn't worship it. Who would want a "sexist," "power-hungry," "thirty- to forty-foot-tall" "old man" with "lightning bolts" looking over him everywhere he went?

These are ugly characteristics, to say the least. To atheists, God is a nasty—one could almost say evil—being. The fact that the atheists believe this negative being *doesn't* exist is a positive sign. To the atheists in this poll, one supernatural creature that is selfish, hateful, and unjust doesn't exist, nor does it have power over us. From this, one might rightly conclude that these atheist respondents were also an optimistic bunch.

At the very least, the nonbelievers were consistent. Their number one response, "nothing," along with the synonyms they selected in the poll ("invisible," "fictitious," "fake"), aligns perfectly with their claim that God does not exist. "Nothing," by definition, does not exist. The believers were also consistent. One of the believers' most popular characteristics for God was the word "everything," and, by definition, "everything" *does* exist.

Thus, the two groups are perfectly consistent within their frames of reference; the problem between atheists and believers occurs when you bring them together and say the word "God." Immediately, the believer pictures a gracious, forgiving, and loving being, and the atheist envisions a controlling, vengeful, and hateful monster—they aren't thinking of the same thing. But if they used their definitions of "God" instead of the actual label, they would essentially agree. Those who say God doesn't exist surely wouldn't claim that love doesn't exist. And, on the other side, believers certainly don't see a hateful, bearded old-timer watching every move they make. When you get down to the definitions, the two groups actually agree!

Reducing the debate to an equation may be helpful. Both believer (B) and atheist (A) think that x, y, and z exist and m, n, and o don't exist. B holds that a specific word equals x, y, and z, and A holds that the same specific word equals m, n, and o. Clearly, in this simplified version of the debate, the core beliefs are the same, it's just the labeling that is off.

	A	**B**	
Exist	x, y, z	x, y, z	**Agreement**
Don't Exist	m, n, o	m, n, o	**Agreement**
Specific Word	m, n, o	x, y, z	**Disagreement**

Fig. 3. Two different people (A annd B) may agree on the existence of certain characteristics, but using an ambiguous word to represent those characteristics may cause disagreement.

As seen in the diagram, atheists and believers are consistent within their own framework, but the two frameworks clash when brought together. Again, what we find in this example is the central problem with communication—one that will be reiterated throughout this book—which is the disconnect between a word and its definition. Both atheists and believers hear roughly the same word in "God," but the two groups apply opposing definitions to that word. People think they understand all that their partner in conversation is saying because he or she is using familiar words; but they may not fully comprehend the meaning behind those words. The differences in meanings between two people, whether subtle or substantial, can have a major impact on a discussion.

An everyday example is the use of the word "good" in a conversation about music between a mother and her teenage child. Let's imagine that, while riding in the family car, teenaged Suzie turns the radio to a piercing rock and roll station, and her mother says that Suzie's music is not good. The daughter says that the music *is* good, and a battle ensues in which the two see who can hit the radio dial more quickly.

In this case, the daughter defines "good" music as music that provides an emotional release, and that can match the angst she feels for having been born in such a horrible world where air conditioning and endless supplies of food are constantly available (I'm sure we can all sympathize). Her mother, on the other hand, classifies music as "good" if it is relaxing and allows her to preserve her hearing. If Suzie and her mother were to be more descriptive in their classification of music, they would find that they agree.

In a more descriptive mood, the mom says, "This music is

difficult to relax to."

The daughter says, "Yes, that's why I love it. It's great for an emotional release. Sometimes I'm just filled with so much angst, and it seems like this singer relates." Ah, if only all teenagers had the capacity to communicate like that.

Mom says, "I can see how you could feel that way, but I'm worried about keeping my hearing, and this isn't helping. Do you want me yelling 'wha?' to you every time you say something? Know what I'm sayin', homegirl?"

And so it is reasonable to assume that a mother and her teenage child could actually agree on music. The words they use are extremely important, however. In order to agree, they must avoid using words that do not have a clear meaning, while also explicitly defining the words they do use. This will keep the two from relying on one ambiguous word and easily falling into an argument.

In the film *Back to the Future*, Michael J. Fox's teenage character Marty McFly goes back in time from 1985 to 1955 and meets up with his friend, Doctor Emmett Brown. Doc doesn't believe that Marty has come from the future, and he questions him about what's going on thirty years in the future.

Doc interrogates his subject, saying, "Then tell me, 'Future Boy,' who's President in the United States in 1985?"

Proud that he knows the answer, Marty responds, "Ronald Reagan."

"Ronald Reagan?! The actor?" Doc chuckles in disbelief. "Then who's *Vice*-President? Jerry Lewis? I suppose Jane Wyman is the First Lady!"

Marty protests. "Whoa! Wait! Doc!"

"And Jack Benny, the Secretary of the Treasury?"

In this case, Marty and Doc are speaking about the same person (Ronald Reagan), who means something completely different to each character. In Doc's 1955 world, Ronald Reagan is an actor (mainly in B movies) whose closest brush with politics was as a witness in the McCarthy hearings on anti-Americanism. To Marty's 1985 character, on the other hand, Ronald Reagan is a successful California Governor and the most popular U.S. president of the century. To Marty, there is nothing abnormal about the notion of Reagan as president; but to Doc, this idea is a joke, simply because his perspective is different from Marty's.

finding meaning

In another great film of the 1980s, *Amadeus*, the antagonist, Salieri, is a composer who envies the genius of Mozart. In one scene, Mozart's wife brings some of Mozart's sheet music to Salieri to have it judged. To me, as to most viewers, the sheet music is just pieces of paper with black markings on top of straight lines, nothing more. I am sheet-music-illiterate. But when Salieri looks at the composition, he hears music, wonderful music; his face shows ecstasy; he is in heaven.

What were just black squiggles to Mozart's wife and to most viewers like me were instruments capable of producing perfect music in Salieri's mind. And this isn't just a cinematic effect used to reveal Mozart's genius; this effect really occurs. Those who can read sheet music can actually hear the notes in their head when they read the black squiggles on the page. They're not hallucinating, nor are they crazy; they're using the same brain functions that most people use when reading words.

But many people can't read sheet music, and, though seeing someone delight in ecstasy while looking at little black squiggles may make the musically illiterate feel like they've been left out of an elite club, I assure you that everyone is part of an elite club, just not that one. Everyone recognizes certain things that others don't, and each person has a unique set of experiences, which lead to a unique perspective and a unique *elite club* of understanding. Breaking into an elite club and understanding its members is just a matter of aligning the perspectives of everyone involved, a task that isn't very difficult.

The number below is extremely important and very meaningful to a lot of people, but it's likely that you won't know why just by looking at it. If you'd like to test whether it means anything to you, give it a try:

0704177612071941

Most people don't know the significance of this number right off the bat, and most won't figure it out if given a short period of time. This is typical of much of the misunderstandings in social discourse, but if a little more information—a little more perspective—is provided, the meaning usually becomes clear. In the case of the above number, most people realize its importance when the word "America" is applied to it. When placed into the context of America, the same numbers that were meaningless just moments ago suddenly reveal Independence Day and the day Pearl Harbor was bombed preceding World War II.

The above example shows how one label (the number) can have two distinct concepts associated with it. When the mind moves the label from meaningless numbers to dates of importance to the United States, a gestalt shift occurs and concurrence is attained. A gestalt shift is the change in conception from one idea to another given the same perception. The afore-mentioned Necker Cube is one example of a gestalt shift—one design can appear two different ways depending on the observer's frame of mind. Both the Necker Cube and the number above illustrate how one stimulus can be interpreted in two completely different ways.

This effect also applies to the real world. I recently overheard two coworkers arguing about a task one asked the other to do. "I told you to email me the specs," one person said.

The other replied, "But I did."

"No, you didn't."

"Yes, I did."

After some explanation, the second person replied with understanding. "Oh, you wanted me to email you the *specs*." This is a classic example of how miscommunication that conveys a different concept than was intended usually results in an unpleasant argument. Luckily, in the case of my coworkers, the second party was open to exploring new ideas of what "specs" meant, which led to the gestalt shift in her mind regarding the topic. The two really agreed all along; they just didn't know it.

he's a bad man

Some readers may be thinking that this isn't a new concept. There are already linguistic concepts that account for the incongruity between words and their meanings, like polysemy and what is considered inversion of meaning. As we will see, however, these concepts do not quite cover the central idea of the theory of concurrence, and the result is that we must invent a new word to describe the idea of different definitions for one word fully.

My friend Patricia decided to *run* errands on a Saturday and she also had the energy to *run* a race later that day. While the common word "run" remains constant in the previous sentence, it has different definitions in the two different contexts. This is called polysemy, the coexistence of multiple definitions for a given word. The dual meaning for the word "run" might be confusing to a three-year-old (or to Paris Hilton), but this dual meaning is not the end of agreement between sensible people. Two people can easily accept that "run" can represent the act of going from store to store to drop off dry cleaning and pick up groceries as well as strapping on a pair of New Balance tennis shoes and breaking a sweat on a three-miler.

In many ways, the polysemy of "run" in the above example is similar to that of the word "God" in the previous section. In both instances, these words have two different meanings. There is one striking difference, however. Most people will allow the word "run" to have multiple meanings, but that same crowd wouldn't consider allowing two definitions for the word "God." This is partly because "God" is a proper noun; but also because the concept of polysemy doesn't quite apply when it comes to social agreement.

The reason for this is that it just doesn't make sense to apply the word "God" to the believers' concept of a loving, graceful, and forgiving being *and* the atheists' idea of a hateful, selfish, and vengeful creation. The difficulty in permitting two definitions for the word "God" arises mainly because the definitions contradict each other. If the word "run" could mean jogging as well as sitting on the couch all day, using the verb would be infinitely more difficult, and would probably lead to some extremely bizarre marketing campaigns by exercise equipment manufacturers.

In addition to having two different definitions, a word can also have its meaning inverted. Inversion of meaning tends to occur with the use of slang (e.g., when "bad" is used to mean "good") and as a result of general rebellion against social constrictions—not because the users really think that bad things are actually good, as in the case of the religious debate above. In Michael Jackson's "Bad" video, for example, the performer extraordinaire uses the slang term "bad" to represent a tough, strong, and talented dancer, all good characteristics to the singer and his viewers. In this case, the only thing truly bad about the video was the fashion statement made by the background dancers. Luckily for us, the spray-painted-bunny-rabbit-with-sunglasses fad went out of style, along with the inversion of the word "bad." Since the meaning of a word is inverted in an effort to contradict mass culture, the inversion loses steam once it seems everyone is using the new inverted term.

But neither polysemy nor inversion of meaning causes arguments. You won't hear a personal assistant and an athlete arguing over whether "run" involves doing errands or jogging. Nor will you hear a senior citizen arguing with a teenager over whether "bad" actually means bad instead of good—the senior usually just gives the teen a funny look and tells him to get a job. On the other hand, atheists and believers really do argue over the word "God." They don't allow multiple definitions for the lone word as in polysemy, and their disagreement isn't fading into history like an eighties fashion tragedy, as it would if it were the result of an inversion of meaning. Words like "God" are a different breed of word altogether.

Since polysemy and inversion of meaning don't quite cover the concept at play in the God debate, I must introduce a new word that should do the trick. A dispective is a fairly straightforward term that represents exactly what's going on in the atheist/believer transaction—and in every seeming disagreement, for that matter. A dispective occurs when two people have different but equally logical perspectives and apply the same label to both.

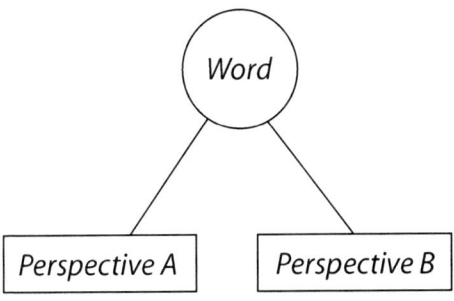

Fig. 4. A dispective occurs when one word is applied to two perspectives.

Couldn't we just use "disagreement" rather than invent a new word? Unfortunately, no. A disagreement implies that two people have a different opinion about the same thing, which isn't the case in a rational discussion. A disagreement must have one right answer and one wrong answer. A dispective is where both explanations are right because they concern different concepts. If this sounds like a nonsensical stew of semantics and terminology, bear with me—help is on the way in the form of a tall, skinny guy and a short, fat one.

who's who?

Costello: Well, then who's on first?
Abbott: Yes.
Costello: I mean the fellow's name.
Abbott: Who.
Costello: The guy on first.
Abbott: Who.
Costello: The first baseman.
Abbott: Who.
Costello: The guy playing . . .
Abbott: Who is on first!
Costello: I'm asking you who's on first.
Abbott: That's the man's name.
Costello: That's whose name?
Abbott: Yes.
Costello: Well go ahead and tell me.
Abbott: That's it.
Costello: That's who?
Abbott: Yes.[5]

I am cracking up right now. The Abbott and Costello act "Who's on First" could be one of the funniest bits in the history of comedy, and the reason, interestingly enough, is because of dispectives. In the act, one character (Costello) tries to find out the names of the players on a baseball team from the future team manager (Abbott). An obvious disconnect occurs when Costello is told the names of the players, which are all common conversational terms. "Who" is the name of the first baseman, but it is also the question used to derive the name of the player. The result is absolute hilarity—Costello gets madder and madder as each one of his questions receives a seemingly inappropriate answer,

Abbott becomes frustrated in trying to convey the obvious, and the conversation became a convoluted dance of precise misunderstanding that's amazing—not to mention side-splitting—to watch.

The normal viewer would get a couple of chuckles out of watching such a performance and be content with that, but I guess I'm not normal because I required a little explanation. Why is it so funny? (And I'm not talking about the outfielder, Why). Why is the confusion people share over the misunderstanding of a word so amusing to the bystander yet so infuriating to the parties involved? E. B. White once said, "Analyzing humor is like dissecting a frog. Few people are interested and the frog dies."[6] But at the risk of killing the frog, I'd like to analyze humor a little.

The science behind what makes us laugh hasn't been thoroughly developed, but there are some interesting ideas in the field, some of which shed light on the concept of social agreement and give credence to the theory of concurrence. An oft-cited definition of what makes us laugh goes back several centuries to 1776, when writer James Beattie described humor as:

> *The view of two or more inconsistent, unsuitable, or incongruous parts or circumstances, considered as united in one complex object or assemblage, or as acquiring a sort of mutual relation from the peculiar manner in which the mind takes notice of them.*[7]

In other words, when we make sense of two things that conflict (e.g., "Who" as a name and a question), we laugh our butts off. It's reasonable, then, to link the dispective defined above with the incongruous parts mentioned in Beattie's definition of humor and apply the result to the "Who's on First" skit. Abbott and Costello each have a unique perspective; in this case, they have different definitions of the word "Who." We viewers realize the incongruity and thus can laugh at it. If Dinesh D'Souza is right and there is an all-knowing God, the God must be rolling with laughter at all the everyday "Who's on First" instances that occur down here.

Usually, however, when we are entrenched in an argument about who hit whom first or what president has the lowest IQ, the conversation is decidedly not funny. People get mad when they disagree. When we're in a heated argument, humor is not the first thing on our minds; when someone tries to make a joke of the situation, tempers flare even more. But Beattie's definition shows that the reason arguments aren't funny to the arguers is because the arguers don't see the connection between the two incongruities—it takes the reconciliation of the arguments to derive humor from the situation.

People do find humor in arguments, however—just ask the actors of the English comedy troupe Monty Python or viewers of the Jerry Springer talk show. In a Monty Python skit, a man enters "The Argument Clinic," where he pays a gentleman for an argument. The paid arguer simply contradicts everything the payee says and takes the money. The bit gets funnier when the two start arguing about what an argument really is:

> *Paying customer: This isn't an argument, this is just contradiction*
> *Arguer: No, it isn't*
> *Paying customer: Yes, it is.*
> *Arguer: Is not.*
> *Paying customer: It is—you just contradicted me [points at the arguer]*
> *Arguer: No, I didn't.*
> *Paying customer: Yes, you did.*

Arguments can even be funny when arguers aren't trying to make us laugh. I'm assuming that's why Jerry Springer was so popular for so long with shows entitled "You Dumped Me at the Alter," "Klanfrontation," and "I Have a Surprise . . . I'm Cheating!" The participants in the half-talk show/half-circus go at each other with vile and venom, and the audience members find it hilarious. Besides being slightly perverse, the audience laughs at the incongruity of the actions onstage.

Studies back up this connection between an argument and comedy. Dean Mobbs and others at Stanford University showed that funny cartoons stimulate a number of regions in the brain, most notably the left side of the temporal-occipital junction (located at the lower back side of the brain), and the left lower inferior frontal gyrus (IFG) and temporal pole (both located in the lower center of the brain).[8] This region—I'll call it the *ah-ha region*—is active when the brain's owner gets a joke, but it's also been linked to conflict resolution and the identification of emotionally important visual cues. From the perspective of the human brain, a joke looks a lot like a resolved argument, which is why Abbott and Costello's skit makes such an impression. Bob Mankoff, cartoon editor of *The New Yorker*, sums it up this way: "When you think rationally, it's A or not A, it's this or it's that. But in comedy, it's always both things."[9] He gives an example: "Think of a cartoon with a guy on the phone saying, 'Thursday's out. How about never? Is never good for you?' It's both rude and polite. The syntax is polite, the message is rude."

Humor and conflict resolution have always been linked in the brain geographically, but in the 1960s, philosophers and science historians attempted to solidify the connection theoretically. In *The Act of Creation*, Arthur Koestler showed that humor, art, and scientific discovery share the same creative process. Koestler coined the term "bisociation," which means the linking of two seemingly unrelated ideas, to explain what goes on in the brain when one is engaged in comedy and scientific discovery. Koestler wrote, "The logical pattern of the creative process is the same in all three cases; it consists in the discovery of hidden similarities."[10] Around the same time, British mathematician and biologist Jacob Bronowski, who studied the creative process, added that, like humor, the progress of science is "the discovery at each step of a new order which gives unity to what had long seemed unlike."[11] In other words, reconciling incongruities is the key to scientific discovery as well as humor, and it's also what helps us in conflict resolution. If the link between these seemingly disparate mental activities seems reasonable to you, it's quite possible you're using the same ah-ha region of the brain to come to that conclusion.

With research like the Mobbs study and others, we're continually improving our understanding of how the brain works. But it's clear at least at this stage that there is an important link between conflict resolution and humor. Eventually, we may learn that a little understanding is all that keeps us from laughing away our differences.

clear as a bell

In 2002, North Carolina teacher Stephanie Bell was required to attend a sensitivity training seminar and to then write a formal letter of apology to the parents of one of her students.[12] Mrs. Bell was also admonished for being insensitive to the diverse population of the school. What infraction did Mrs. Bell commit? In reference to a literary character, she used the word "niggardly," which for centuries has been a synonym of "miserly" and "stingy." The word also has the dishonor of sounding very similar to a nasty racial epithet that has a long history of enraging people. The offended student wasn't hurt by the idea of a stingy character, of course; she was offended by her misinterpretation of the word Mrs. Bell used.

While my goal is not to defend or condemn either the teacher or the student in this matter, this incident is a great example of how simple misunderstandings (dispectives) can arise and cause real problems in the world. The misunderstanding in the Bell case is just about on par with the misunderstanding in the Abbott and Costello skit. The teacher was talking about penny pinching and the student heard hate mongering. But no one was laughing in North Carolina.

Another case of unintended implications occurred when I made the mistake of giving someone an unwelcome nickname. In the late 1990s, I developed a promotional poster series for the Indiana University football team. Each poster was to have a designated player's name displayed with images of his athletic prowess superimposed in the letters. The first player in the series was to be the phenomenal option quarterback Antwaan Randle El. It was decided to print his first name on the poster, but, because "Antwaan" was too long to fit, I christened him with the nickname 'Twaan. Once the poster was approved and sent off to print, some coworkers who were more attuned to pop culture than I informed me that the name 'Twaan was associated with more effeminate males, like Damon Wayans' character in the television show *In Living Color*—not something I wanted to imply for an athlete in a masculine sport like football. Needless to say, the posters flopped.

The confusion in both the Bell case and the poster incident was caused by an incongruity in the definition of a term, but the miscommunication wasn't intended. Some speakers, however, plan such miscommunication intentionally. Politicians are particularly talented at this skill and most use ambiguity as an art. A British study in 2003 showed that politicians in general fail to say what they mean.[13] In fact, the study found that, when fielding questions, politicians answered the question they had been asked only 46 percent of the time. Of course, this isn't a new discovery. Politicians have been known to be some of the most slippery speakers in all of society, ever since Brutus tried to justify Caesar's assassination by saying that he "loved Rome more."

It's no wonder politicians are so evasive; they are trying to please a majority of the electorate with everything they say, and that's a difficult task. In addition, questions are sometimes framed in a lose-lose way so that a straightforward answer will be damaging no matter what the politician's position. We can all relate to a politician in cases like these, though. If you've ever skirted around a tough question because you didn't want to hurt someone's feelings, then you are guilty of being an everyday equivocator. "Did you like the patchwork sweater I got you for your birthday?" your great-aunt Mildred may ask. "Oh, you're so thoughtful! That was so nice of you" is your ambiguous reply.

One way modern politicians attempt to equivocate is by simply not talking about controversial issues. A Barack Obama commercial that aired during the summer of 2008, for instance, showed how an ambiguous message could be used to stimulate support. The television spot showed a diverse population expressing its desire to vote for the presidential candidate simply based on *hope*. "I hope for a president that I can look up to," one of the speakers proclaims. "Hope is the reason I'm voting for this guy," another says. The ad never explains what Obama would do in office; it doesn't elucidate his past accomplishments; and it doesn't even show the candidate kissing any babies. It does, however, associate the candidate with the concept of hope, an equivocation by any standard, though one that turned out to be very effective. After all, who can argue with the concept of hope? Obama capitalized on this positive ambiguity, going from a political outsider in 2007 to president of the United States within the span of a few months all based on his simple message of hope.

Although ambiguity may save great-aunt Mildred from bitter tears and some politicians from a divisive electorate, equivocation is not good for communication or society in general. In fact, it's one of the most damaging fallacies in logic to occur in social discourse. Former president Clinton found this out when, in an act of equivocation, he claimed that he did not have sexual relations with Monica Lewinsky, thus leading to the most convoluted Grand Jury testimony ever centered around the definition of the word "is":

> *It depends on what the meaning of the word "is" is. If the—if he—if "is" means "is and never has been," that is not—that is one thing. If it means there is none, that was a completely true statement . . . Now, if someone had asked me on that day, are you having any kind of sexual relations with Ms. Lewinsky, that is, asked me a question in the present tense, I would have said no. And it would have been completely true.* [14]

Never has such a simple word become so confusing! But ambiguity doesn't just haunt improprieties in the Oval Office; it also haunts presidents on naval aircraft carriers. When President Bush landed a jet fighter on the USS Abraham Lincoln and declared that "major combat operations in Iraq have ended," he did so in front of a banner that read "Mission Accomplished."[15] This optimistic attitude may strike many voters as odd, seeing as how the majority of military casualties in Iraq have occurred since that publicity stunt.[16] Bush, like Clinton, used ambiguity to appear morally justified; in the end, this ambiguity hurt him badly—perhaps even more so than did Clinton's. Each incident gave these presidents' opponents fuel to criticize them and spend a great deal of energy sorting out the equivocation.

Returning to the 2008 election, another catchword used often, first by Obama, then by John McCain, was "change"—a word most candidates for non-incumbent parties use to capitalize on any dissatisfaction within the electorate. Obama's website and most of his campaign posters proudly proclaimed, "Change we can believe in" or "Obama for change." In McCain's acceptance speech at the 2008 Republican National Convention, he proclaimed, "Change is coming!" Change can be positive as well as inevitable, but is change always good? A poll conducted by Amelior Institute showed how the word can imply completely different ideas. When asked what Obama's message of change meant, some respondents replied that it meant a return to "the rights embedded in our Constitution" or the straightforward "different from how things are now." Others saw change as less benign. One respondent saw it as "change from a representative democracy to a socialist society, maybe a banana republic." Another read change as "what I'll have left in my wallet when I'm done paying taxes." It's clear, at least in the case of the ambiguous word "change," that political talk should be a bit more specific if it is to avoid confusion and disagreement.

We should give all of the above politicians the benefit of the doubt and assume that they intended to present the truth to us. But we should also be aware of the difficulty that the separation of labels and their meanings cause in language. A classic Groucho Marx line in the movie *Animal Crackers* makes light of the problem. He said, "One morning I shot an elephant in my pajamas. How he got into my pajamas I'll never know."[17] Ambiguity can be funny in the case of a misplaced modifier, as in a Marx Brothers movie, but in the case of a misunderstood schoolteacher, it can be life-changing; in the case of a Bill Clinton testimony or a George Bush publicity stunt, it can be disastrous.

In order for everyone to agree, ambiguity must be reduced to a minimum. So when politicians like Barack Obama or John McCain talk generically about "change" or "hope," it behooves the listener to question exactly what kind of change or hope they're talking about.

define your terms

Ambiguity in political ads or stump speeches may lead to misplaced support for a particular candidate, but ambiguity in a heated debate can lead to animosity and can further the crippling moral dualism that's so prevalent today. One particularly ambiguous term that was used throughout the 2008 presidential campaign was the term "surge," used with regard to the Iraq war. The surge was discussed during the lone vice-presidential debate between Joseph Biden and Sarah Palin.

Governor Palin extolled the success of the counterinsurgency plan, saying, "The surge worked" and "the surge principles that have worked in Iraq need to be implemented in Afghanistan."[18] She then pitted herself and her running mate, John McCain, against the opposition, saying, "You guys opposed the surge" and "Barack Obama still can't admit the surge works." Senator Biden did not deny Palin's accusation and in fact went on to give proof as to why he thought the surge would not work in Afghanistan. He said, "The fact is that our commanding general in Afghanistan said today that a surge—the surge principles used in Iraq will not—well, let me say this again now—our commanding general in Afghanistan said the surge principle in Iraq will not work in Afghanistan."[18]

It had become clear throughout the campaign that McCain and Palin were pro-surge for Iraq and Afghanistan, and Obama and Biden were anti-surge. But the two debaters and perhaps a good deal of their audience also forgot to do one thing before debating the surge—they forgot to define what "the surge" meant. Throughout the entire conversation on the topic, the surge was never clearly explained; its meaning was just assumed by all parties. The result was a dispective of the term "surge" and the inevitable confusion that arises from such miscommunication.

If you look up the Iraq troop surge on Wikipedia, the online encyclopedia, you'll find a description of the surge as the addition of 20,000 more troops to the theater of Iraq, a reference to longer troop deployment in some cases, and President Bush's goal of helping "Iraqis clear and secure neighborhoods, [helping] them protect the local population, and [helping] ensure that the Iraqi forces left behind are capable of providing the security."[19]

Now, if Biden was so opposed to applying the surge to Afghanistan, why would he say that we need more troops in Afghanistan? "We need government-building," he explained. "We need to spend more money on the infrastructure in Afghanistan." The plan that Biden was promoting for Afghanistan was precisely the plan laid out by Wikipedia in its definition of the Iraq surge. Yet Biden claimed that he opposed a surge in the Afghanistan conflict. I don't think that Biden was intentionally being contradictory; I think that he forgot to define his terms, and his debating partner didn't help. Like the participants in the debate on religion, these political debaters, Biden and Palin, seemingly opposed each other with regard to a central idea of the campaign; but, as it turns out, they only disagreed on the definition of a term, not on the correct policy to implement.

The term "surge" is an example of one word that is unwittingly applied to two different ideas—a typical dispective. And while the results of the disagreement may be blatantly obvious in the animosity created between the opposing debaters, the source of the problem can be obscure, as is demonstrated in a conversation between Dwight Schrute and Jim Halpert in an episode of the television show *The Office*. In it, Dwight explains in a creepily serious voice that, in the case of a violent encounter with a zombie, "nothing is better to have at your disposal than a crossbow." Jim, amused that anyone would go to such lengths to think up a sentence like that, asks, "What about your authentic samurai sword that you hide in your cubical desk drawer?" Dwight counters with a condescending, "I guess a samurai sword is better than nothing."

Jim, in an ever-present mood to tease Dwight, spots another opportunity to do so. "Well," Jim says, "if a samurai sword is better than *nothing* and *nothing* is better than a crossbow, then a samurai sword must be better than a crossbow." At which point

Dwight looks accusingly at Jim before telling him to stop playing Jedi mind tricks on him.

What Dwight fell for in this scenario—and what many of us fall for on a daily basis—is the application of multiple definitions to one word. In this case, "nothing" refers to "the other weapons" in one sentence and "no weapon" in the other; but when both definitions are applied to the one label, confusion abounds.

Thus, reason dictates that if we come to a point in conversation at which a disagreement is imminent, we should simply ask for clarification. When a coworker tells you that Cleveland is a much more beautiful place to live than San Diego, ask to see the pictures. When a friend claims that Allen Iverson was the best basketball player ever when it's clear that Michael Jordan holds the title, ask the friend if he's seen his *airness* in action. And when someone disagrees with you on the success of the troop surge, make sure you have the same definition of "surge" before you go at each other's throats.

The point of defining the terms used in a discussion is to get roughly the same perspective as the person with whom you're conversing. There's no sense is saying that Michael Jordan was the greatest basketball player ever if the person listening has never seen an NBA Final. The other party will either take you at your word or pass your claim off as useless information. If the other party has a good idea of basketball but has seen very little of Michael Jordan, it's possible that he or she could anoint another player as the greatest of all time. Only when you and your companion have witnessed the same pieces of evidence will you be able to rationally discuss the topic.

Defining your subject matter as a way to overcome disagreements may seem obvious, but it is rarely done. As in the debates between the believers and atheists, and the Democrats and Republicans, many discussions become heated and antagonistic when definitions aren't stipulated at the outset. Does God exist? Was the surge successful? These questions both beg the real issues: what is God and what is the surge? If we can agree on the definitions of those major ideas, the question of existence and of success will fall logically in line.

Defining your subject matter could be an extremely lengthy process, however. In the case above, Governor Palin would have had to explain exactly what the troop surge entailed—how many troops, what interaction with Iraqi leaders, and how much more money—in order to get on the same page with Biden. Most people don't have the time or the patience to relay such details, especially when their debate is given a two-minute time limit. This is why we label concepts and summarize large ideas with small names in the first place: to save time in conveying our ideas. But the result of using arbitrary terms like "surge" instead of clear definitions is confusion and usually a bitter opposition or simply an agreement to disagree.

The surge and basketball debates described above are examples of what I previously described as a dispective. In these instances, it wasn't that the debaters completely understood each other's perspectives and genuinely felt that the other person was wrong. In the cases above, as with Rosie and Elisabeth, and Hitchens and D'Souza, the participants simply applied two different perspectives to the same word. Unfortunately, with the complexity of experience that we each have, this clash of perspectives is pretty much inevitable in any discussion. Unless two people have had the exact same experiences throughout their lives, their definitions for words are going to vary, sometimes dramatically.

Acknowledging that words can have different definitions, however, we can attempt to overcome the problem of miscommunication. Instead of assuming that everyone shares your perspective, assume the opposite and explain your perspective to facilitate the conversation. If one label or word in a discussion seems to cause disagreement, don't assume the other person is crazy or evil; ask for an explanation or a definition of the label or word in question. "If you wish to converse with me," French philosopher and writer Voltaire once penned, "define your terms."[20] And so we should if we are at all interested in communicating effectively. When we acknowledge the incongruity between our words and our thoughts, and define our terms, we will find that agreement comes a lot easier.

onward

In the year 1900, a British scientist, William Thompson Kelvin, proclaimed to the world, "There is nothing new to be discovered in physics now. All that remains is more and more precise measurement."[21] That absurd statement didn't stop the King from knighting Kelvin a few years later, and it surely didn't stop Albert Einstein from discovering relativity a few years after that, thus altering the entire physics landscape. Despite Kelvin's doubtful claim, the science world was ready for a big overhaul, and Einstein was just the Swiss patent clerk to instigate it.

Physicists at that time had taken all the data that was available from experiments and theories dating back to the 1700s and crowned Newtonian physics the reigning sovereign over the science. Then Einstein came on to the scene and took roughly the same empirical data but came away with a completely different concept of reality. Whereas popular physics in 1900 held that space was a fixed and stationary entity, Einstein saw space as dynamic according to what is contained within it.

The science historian Thomas Kuhn called this monumental change in scientific conception from Newtonian to Einsteinian physics a paradigm shift (similar to the gestalt shift mentioned earlier). He held that under certain circumstances, any scientific field may alter the way it looks at its data, thus producing significant advances; for example, the Copernican revolution, which removed the Earth from the center of the universe in scientific theory, and the Einsteinian shift mentioned above. An important aspect of this shift is that the raw information—the perception—is the same; what changes is what people do with that raw information—the conception.

Kuhn used an optical illusion similar to the Necker Cube described in the Introduction to demonstrate how a paradigm shift can cause a person to see one image in two different ways. The optical illusion was the duck/rabbit illustration, which depicts either a thick-beaked mallard or a fuzzy hare, depending on

Fig. 5. The same illustration can easily be conceived as a duck or a rabbit, depending on the viewer's intent.

what you want to see.

A paradigm shift, which can be demonstrated with an optical illusion, reflects exactly what goes on when the ah-ha region of the brain is activated during scientific discovery and, as shown above, when a joke is told, as well. But the ah-ha region is only active when the incongruities in a given situation are resolved, as is the case when a viewer of the "Who's on First" skit realizes that "Who" is a name as well as a question. On the other side of the coin, the incongruity that isn't resolved can result in bitter feuds (as in the God debate), angry coworkers (as in the case of the Bush debaters), and impeachment (as in the Clinton equivocation).

All disagreements are essentially conversations in which incongruities haven't been resolved. Two people use one word without considering that it may have two meanings—they assume that their single perspective applies to everyone. This dispective, then, is the central problem in communication; but it's easily averted. By acknowledging the incongruity and simply defining the terms of our discussion, we trigger the ah-ha region in our brains and arrive at a paradigm shift.

This shift will inevitably point to an ultimate truth. Kuhn said that when a scientific paradigm is replaced, the new one is always better, not just different. This is an ultimate truth involved in the concept of concurrence. But before we can attempt to clarify concurrence, we must look at the other side of the perception/conception coin. We've examined what happens when people use one label to represent two concepts; now we must look at what happens when two labels are used to represent one concept.

part II

buddhism, bare breasts, and bureaucracy

Around 350 AD, an Indian prince named Josaphat was born into wealth and privilege in the kingdom of his father, Abenner, which had recently been inundated with Christian missionaries.[1] King Abenner rejected the new faith and even persecuted the followers of Christianity, thus he was shocked to learn that his astrologers unanimously predicted that his son, Josaphat, would one day become a Christian. King Abenner would have none of this, so he essentially imprisoned his son, restricting him from leaving the palace grounds.

Josaphat grew up sheltered from the outside world and all of the suffering that inhabited it. And though he had everything he could ask for—wealth, women, and food—Josaphat felt as if there was something missing in his life. So one day the prince escaped from his palatial prison and set out to explore. Upon entering the real world, the sheltered young man was shocked to find sickness, death, and pain throughout the land.

On his journey, the prince met a hermit named Barlaam, who was happy despite his poverty. Josaphat inquired as to how Barlaam was able to overcome such a lowly state of existence, and Barlaam answered that Jesus Christ enabled him, through his earthly body, to embrace the angelic. Josaphat was immediately convinced, and he converted to Christianity on the spot. The prince later helped spread the word of Christianity throughout the subcontinent, and both he and Barlaam were canonized as saints by the Catholic Church and honored by many other Christian sects.

Most historians attribute this story of Barlaam and Josaphat to St. John of Damascus, but there is a good deal of uncertainty about the true author and the exact year it was written. One thing is pretty clear to historians, however, and that's that Josaphat's story is nearly identical to the story of Siddhartha Gautama, the Buddha of the ancient Indian religion. In Buddhist texts, Siddhartha was born a prince in an Indian kingdom and astrologers and scholars predicted that Siddhartha would become a mighty king or a great holy man. Attempting to perfectly educate his son, the king sheltered Siddhartha from the horrors of real life for twenty-nine years; then Siddhartha ventured out and met two hermit teachers, under whom he learned meditative consciousness. He eventually became enlightened and took the name Buddha.

In this part of *Everyone Agrees*, I intend to show that different groups of people use different terms for the same concept, a phenomenon I've termed *monospective*. A monospective is the opposite of a dispective, in which one word has two definitions. In the case of a monospective, two words have one definition. Christianity and Buddhism applied different labels to the story of a man learning the ways of the world, just as people every day use different labels to describe the same things. Anytime this happens, the result is artificial divisiveness.

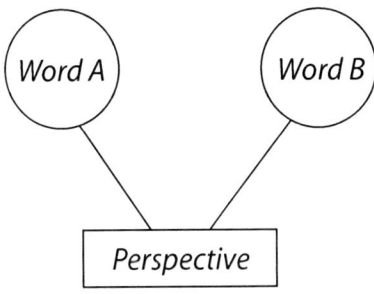

Fig. 6. A monospective occurs when two parties apply two different words to a single perspective.

We will see how monospectives cause trouble in communication between the world's religions and between atheists and believers. The concept of the monospective also helps us to understand general belief systems among diverse populations. We'll see how sexual morality can be consistent in societies as disparate as Renaissance Europe and the modern society that produced the notorious wardrobe malfunction during a Super Bowl halftime show, despite the outward expressions of that morality. The monospective also illustrates a concept called Schelling points, which are focal points or solutions that a group of people tend to use even without communicating with each other—we'll see how. The fact that people don't recognize that they agree when they use different terms contributes to the moral dualism described in the introduction. Acknowledging the monospective will no doubt lead us on the path to concurrence.

believe it or not

It's not clear what copyright infringements were violated in St. John's writing of Josaphat and Barlaam, but since the story is so similar to that of Siddhartha, one can almost claim that the Buddha was actually canonized as a saint in the Catholic Church. St. Josaphat's name is even derived from the Persian *Budsaif*, which comes from *Bodhisattva* (the Buddhist term for a person who is able to reach nirvana). Some religious exclusionists may see this as treading closely on heresy—the Church would never canonize a leader of *another* religion. But why shouldn't it? Is it not possible or even probable that a man renowned for his deep compassion for all living things and his love of knowledge (Buddha) could be praised by a Church that promotes the same things?

As many have come to realize over the centuries, there are endless similarities between Christianity and Buddhism, and the story of Barlaam and Josaphat is just one element shared by the two religions. Both Buddha and Jesus are said to have undergone a virgin birth[2] and to have begun their celebrated prophesying around the age of thirty. The story of the prodigal son, found in the Gospel of Luke, reflects a similar story found in *Saddharma Pundarika Sutra*, the preaching of the Buddha. Buddhism and Christianity also both focus on spreading peace, loving fellow humans (including one's enemies), and the incomprehensibility of God.[3] In fact, there are so many similarities between the two belief systems that large organizations, such as the Society for Buddhist-Christian Studies, have formed in order to facilitate and explain the connection.

Meditation is another practice that is central to both Buddhism and Christianity. Techniques to encourage mindfulness, concentration, and tranquility are at the core of Buddhist practice. And for centuries, Christians have used what they call a Prayer of Silence, which encompasses the same techniques as meditation. William Johnston, an Irish Jesuit and active participant in the Christian/Buddhist dialogue, has shared a story about meditation in his book *Christian Zen*. When a Zen teacher asks him what he's experiencing while he's meditating, Johnston replies that he's "sitting silently in the presence of God." The teacher continues, asking, "Your God is everywhere?" When Johnston replies in the affirmative, the teacher is encouraged. "Very good! Very good!" he exclaims. "Continue this way . . . and eventually you will find that God will disappear and only Johnston-san will remain." Shocked at the seeming heresy, the student replies that God will not disappear; Johnston might well disappear and leave only *God*. The teacher smiles and replies, "Yes, yes, it is the same thing."[4]

Andrew Newberg and his late colleague Eugene d'Aquilli of the University of Pennsylvania solidified the meditation connection in several religions in 2003.[5] They found that brain scans of Franciscan nuns engaged in intense prayer matched closely the scans of Buddhist monks during meditation. They also found that prayer and meditation coincided with a large drop in activity in the parietal lobe, which is located in the upper back area of the brain (just north of the ah-ha region), and an increase in activity in the right prefrontal cortex, which is located behind the forehead. The parietal lobe is usually associated with navigation and spatial orientation, and the decrease in activity may give the feeling of being one with the universe. The prefrontal cortex is heavily involved with planning, and it's believed that activity in that region may explain the feeling of deep concentration induced by prayer or meditation.

Links between other religions are more obvious. The three major Abrahamic religions all share reverence for the Hebrew Bible—the Old Testament—and there are further connections between the three belief systems. Associations between those major monotheistic religions are abundant, including belief in the one true God of Abraham and such specific details as the location of the final judgment, which will happen, according to most Jews, Christians, and Muslims, at the Valley of Kidron on the eastern side of Jerusalem.

Buddhism and Hinduism also share many similarities, as the Buddha was born into a Hindu tradition much like Jesus was born into a Jewish one. In addition, Hinduism (the third largest religion on Earth by number of adherents[6]) shares many of the same beliefs as the Abrahamic religions, such as heaven (Moska), one supreme God, and a judgment day that brings on the end of the world. Hinduism specifically shares with Christianity the belief of a divinely incarnated Son of God (Jesus in Christianity and Krishna in Hinduism).[7] We can see with this brief smattering of examples that similarities abound in the world's religions. As George Bernard Shaw once wrote, "There is only one religion, though there are a hundred versions of it."[8]

While there is a wealth of similarities between the various religions of the world, a religious exclusionist would say that the stories may be comparable, but the resultant morals or conclusions of those narratives are vastly different. As in the above story, Josaphat found *Jesus*, and his mirror in ancient India, Siddhartha Gautama, found *enlightenment*. The skeptic will claim that these are two vastly different concepts—but are they? If you ask a handful of Buddhists what enlightenment entails, they will detail an experience of escape from material desires and an awareness of all that is, accompanied by "the Great Compassion," which fills the enlightened person's heart with the joy and suffering of the world. If you ask a group of Christians what it means to find Jesus, they will describe an awakening of consciousness and an unleashing of all earthly ties met with unending love. To an alien hearing about the two experiences for the first time, it's conceivable that they could very well be seen as identical phenomena. As the teacher in William Johnston's story reveals, the words may be different, but the experience they're describing is the same.

I'm reminded of this connection every time I log on to the popular social networking website Facebook. On it, I often see my religious friends offering prayers for other friends, and I also see my non-religious friends sending out "good karma" to each other. It seems clear to me that the two behaviors are really one—both my religious and non-religious friends are spreading good will and wishes around.

It appears that, with the religions mentioned above and the good wishes on Facebook, people agree, even though their words don't. Yet, despite all of the similarities between the world's religions, if you sat a strict Buddhist or Jew down with a strict Christian or Muslim, the adherents would likely reject the other faith out of hand. After all, that's why they associate with the religion they do—because they think the others are wrong. This is where the concept of a monospective rears its ugly head. People assume that because they have different *names* for their ideas, they also have different *ideas*; but this isn't the case. Christians and Buddhists do the same thing during prayer or meditation; the Abrahamic religions all agree on the same foundation; Hinduism shares many traits with all the other major religions; and Facebook users are doing the same thing whether they pray for one another or send each other good karma.

Monospectives don't just occur in religious debates, though. Studies show that they pop up in everyday situations, such as when making financial decisions—places we would never think to look. A study conducted by Benedetto De Martino at University College London showed that participants made risky financial decisions based on the labels used in a given scenario, not on their actual monetary gain.[9] In the study, subjects started with $100 and had to decide to go home with only $40 or gamble the $40 for a chance of earning the full $100 reward. Subjects chose to gamble much more often when the first option was labeled *losing* $60 as opposed to *keeping* $40. The situation was the exact same in both cases except for one label, but that label alone made a dramatic impact on the participants' willingness to take risky measures and gamble away a sure reward.

If we can learn to avoid the problems associated with applying two labels to one idea, we will find that we all agree much more than we thought. After all, $40 is the same amount of money whether it is labeled as losing $60 or keeping $40. Similarly, attaining oneness with your inner being is the same thing whether it is called praying or meditating. Much of the time, we all agree; we just don't call it that.

the scientific god

For decades, Michael Persinger has put a helmet on thousands of subjects and revealed to them the presence of God. No, Persinger isn't a cult leader bringing in naïve souls willing to succumb to magic tricks. He is actually a scientist at Laurentain University in

Ontario, and he has dedicated much of his work to understanding the physical aspect of religious experience.

The helmet he uses, dubbed the "God Helmet," generates weak electromagnetic fields and focuses them on areas of the brain that have been associated with religious experiences. Persinger's subjects entered his experiment thinking the helmet was meant to help them relax, but they usually walked away having felt a sensed presence (the feeling of someone near them though no one was) or a profound cosmic bliss that revealed a universal truth.[10] Each subject, then, naturally applied his or her own cultural and religious language to that feeling; some called it God, others Buddha, and still others termed it a benevolent presence or the wonder of the universe.[11] One of the upshots of this experiment is that Persinger showed that in the real world, everyone is quite probably labeling the same religious experiences with different terms. If the Irish Jesuit Johnston and his Zen teacher from above both put on the God Helmet, it's likely they would experience the same thing but call it something different.

The same applies to Buddhists and Christians in everyday practice. However, I'm not arguing that Buddhism is an Eastern form of Christianity or that followers of Jesus are really following the Buddha. I am saying that the religious behavior and the core goals of both worldviews line up with each other quite nicely.

Eckhart Tolle, the popular author and spiritual teacher whose ideas Oprah Winfrey can't seem to get enough of, shows the similarities between Jesus' teachings and those of the Buddha in his book *The New Earth*. Buddha and Jesus were, to Tolle, messengers of a new awakening—an awakening that has yet to fully flower in humanity. Throughout the book, Tolle combines the concepts of both religions so as to blur the distinctions between them, as he did early on by linking the Buddhist concept of *dukkha* (suffering, unsatisfactoriness) and the Christian idea of original sin.[12]

Noting the similarities between the major world religions is one thing, but what can we make of the fifteen or so percent[13] of the world's population who consider themselves atheist or non-religious? They, by definition, think that the central belief of the other 85 percent of the world's population is a mistake. So, one might rightly suppose that there are no similarities between the atheist mindset and the religious one. Quite a few scientists would disagree, though. Harvard biologist Marc Hauser wrote in his book *Moral Minds*, "Across a suite of moral dilemmas and testing situations, Jews, Catholics, Protestants, Sikhs, Muslims, atheists, and agnostics deliver the same judgments."[14] With a brief flushing out of the religious/atheist debate, I intend to show that the two groups have a lot more in common than that. In fact, they may just agree on the central concept of God, though the terms they use to describe that concept are different.

First and foremost in the debate, we must agree that it's pointless to argue about that which is beyond our ability to know (i.e., supernatural entities). Atheists ask believers to prove God's existence, and the reply usually consists of a loose translation of Christian geneticist Francis Collins' excuse that "God's existence is outside of science's ability to really weigh in."[15] Of course we can't prove the existence of God if God is incomprehensible—by definition, that would be impossible. Atheists fall into this trap just as much as believers do, however, when they claim that an incomprehensible God doesn't exist. We can postulate and guess all we care to, but at the end of the day, it's useless to positively assert anything that is incomprehensible. Does that mean that an incomprehensible God does or doesn't exist? No, it just points to the futility of discussing something of that nature.

One striking quality about an intelligent atheist argument is that it usually allows for some sort of higher being, which would seemingly allow room for God. As biologist Richard Dawkins stated in an interview when asked about the possibility of God, "There could be something incredibly grand and incomprehensible and beyond our present understanding."[15] That definition just happens to agree nicely with the common believer's definition of God, but it reverts back to the original problem of discussing something we can't know anything about—what's the point?

Second, despite the difference in terminology, both people involved in the religion debate must concede that they don't know *everything*. A believer can't claim to know everything about God, especially if God is omniscient, because doing so would make him omniscient, as well; in which case he would be so busy buying winning lottery tickets that he wouldn't have time to argue about God's existence. Likewise, atheists can't claim to know everything, either. Despite a century of dedicated thought and analysis, science still hasn't discovered the nature of the universe before the Big Bang—the accepted scientific beginning to the universe as we know it—or whether the Big Bang was, in fact, the origin of the universe in the first place. And we still don't understand the nature of consciousness. In fact, there is always something to be learned—especially with regard to a concept as large as God and the nature of the universe.

In this respect, the atheist and believer are both certainly uncertain. They know some things about their subject, but, naturally, no one can be said to know everything. This concept is tied to the term "agnostic," which is, by definition, a person who is uncertain about claims of ultimate knowledge.[16] With regard to God and the nature of the universe, we can all be said to be agnostic. And, ironically, our uncertainty only becomes apparent the older and wiser we get. As Oscar Wilde once wrote, "I am not young enough to know everything."[17]

When we strip away all the discussion about that which can't ever be known and admit that no one knows everything, it's easy to see how the two sides of the God debate actually agree. Believers and atheists both acknowledge that there was a beginning of the universe, for example, and that people can experience a feeling of unity with that universe. Atheists call these the Big Bang and electromagnetic waves (like those artificially created in the Persinger experiment), and believers call them acts of God. Is there anything inherently different in these concepts besides their names? No—the beginning of the universe and the sensation of unity are typical monospectives in which one shared concept is given two different labels.

Let's investigate further. We know that different religious adherents experienced a monospective from the God Helmet, calling the same sensation either "God" or "Buddha." But did atheists also feel the same thing? Yes. When atheists or nonbelievers put on the God Helmet, they didn't simply reject the same experiences that believers felt; as Dr. Persinger reported, atheists felt the extraordinary experiences like everyone else. "However," he wrote, "they differ from believers by their attribution of the experience. They simply explain it in terms of brain function."[18]

Are believers wrong, then, in attributing a seeming brain function to a specific thing like God? Hitchens, the atheist hero from the introduction, thinks not. He has given a name to the same sensations atheists may feel under the God Helmet; his term is the *numinous*. He explained in an interview that we humans have a feeling of awe and a sense of wonder when we stand on a mountaintop or look at pictures of galaxies from the Hubble telescope—things that are beyond ourselves. To Hitchens, that's the numinous. What differentiates the numinous from God in this situation is not obvious to me, and it's not clear that Hitchens knows the difference either.

It is clear that people who labeled the sensations they felt under the God Helmet to be the result of an actual god were mistaken. The sensations were a direct result of electromagnetic waves being applied to certain parts of the brain. But they were attributed to God because the subjects had a preconceived notion of God. So where did that initial concept come from? We can be sure that it didn't come from the helmet—it must have come through previous experiences that were similar to those sensations they felt while wearing the helmet. Dr. Newberg wrote that, throughout their lives, religious people may have experienced the same sensations as they did under the God Helmet. When the believer returns to the normal state of being after the Godlike sensation, the brain attempts to integrate the phenomenon with common experience. "When weird things happen," Newberg wrote, "the causal functions of our brain try to make sense out of them—to give them a reason, a cause."[19] Some people call the sensations simply brain functions; Hitchens would call it the numinous; and some people, through their cultural influences, name this cause God.

The main contention atheists have with religious nomenclature still remains: yes, there was a beginning to the universe as we know it; and yes, we sometimes feel awe; but why make the quantum leap and attribute both to God? This comes down to the commonly accepted difference between believers and atheists: believers have faith in the unknowable and atheists require proof for their beliefs. Or do they? I don't want to burst anyone's bubble, but the answer is no.

Atheists criticize religious adherents for putting blind faith into a series of claims made by people in white robes with funny staffs. Instead, they put blind faith into a series of claims made by people in white lab coats with funny instruments. Okay, the analogy is a little bit of a stretch, but the similarities are still valid. The fact that we humans—even the brightest of us—can't know everything means that there are times when we must put faith in others. When a doctor in a white coat and a stethoscope scribbles something on a piece of paper and tells us to take it to the pharmacy, we trust that he's conducted the appropriate tests and that he's acting in our best interest in prescribing a particular drug; but we can't be sure. In other words, we have faith in the doctors who treat us and the druggists who give us our pills. Most of us don't know the first thing about chemistry or the science behind pharmaceuticals, so it can rationally be said that our trust in the medical profession is blind faith. However, one would be hard pressed to find someone willing to condemn a medical patient based on his or her blind faith.

On the flip side, most would say that religious adherents don't require proof in the way that an atheist does. But if the goal of religion is to adhere to a moral code and to live a better and happier life, the proof of the pudding is in the eating. Study after study has shown that religion is healthy for one's mental state and level of happiness.[20] Dr. Harold Koenig, a psychologist and co-director of the Center for Spirituality, Theology and Health at Duke University, said, "Generally, religious people have a positive view of the world. They believe they are here for a reason. They see a purpose and a meaning in their life and have hope."[21] So while proof of the viability of religion doesn't look like scientific data, it does exist.

Despite the difference in nomenclature between believers and atheists, it is clear that both have the capacity to and actually do experience the same phenomena. When we remove talk about things we can't know and accept that we don't know everything, we can start to come together, even on issues like religion. Moreover, when scrutinized, it's clear that the typical differences that separate atheists and believers—faith and proof—actually apply to both groups of people. In the arena of religion, it appears that we all agree on the concept, just not the name.

keeping abreast on things

On February 1, 2004, nearly 90 million Americans were shocked when they saw a female nipple (belonging to pop star Janet Jackson) on national television during the Super Bowl halftime show. Viewers were so shocked that they complained a record 200,000 times to the Federal Communications Commission the following week about the complete disregard of morality presented by the show's producers, and the furor spurred a controversy over who was to blame for the wardrobe malfunction. The controversy, dubbed "Nipplegate,"[22] got everyone involved, and the story occupied the media outlets for days. The nipple exposure ended up costing CBS, the network that aired the Super Bowl, a dear $550,000.

The wardrobe malfunction wasn't the most intriguing aspect

of the controversy, though; what was most interesting was that in the wake of an exposed breast on national television, the otherwise pornographic and sexually violent extravaganza that led up to it was relatively ignored. The nipple exposure was the climax of a carefully choreographed dance burlesque that included dozens of constantly gyrating and scantily-clad extras, crotch-grabbing rappers, and dance moves that persistently imitated sex. Any rational person could have described the entire show as soft porn. But viewers weren't particularly disturbed by the indecent physical behavior throughout the show until there was partial nudity involved. Why should they have been? They had been inundated with nationally televised dance acts by the likes of Britney Spears and Janet's brother Michael Jackson for years, all of which featured enough gyrating and crotch-grabbing to give viewers nightmares for weeks.

For some reason, in 2004, the raunchy dance style had been deemed appropriate by society—probably for the same reason that nudity had been deemed inappropriate. It was okay to simulate sex as long as the participants were fully clothed, and it was okay to grab private parts as long as they actually remained private. This bizarre morality may seem inconsistent when looked at objectively, but such was the state of society around the time of the 2004 Super Bowl, and it still is. Based solely on Nipplegate, some may rightly claim that we're losing all sense of morals, but I will attempt to show that the controversy reveals that our morals are still alive and kicking, but that the manifestations of those morals are completely different than those of our predecessors.

Cultural norms have changed dramatically throughout history—for proof, just take a stroll through your local art museum. If there is a realist modern painting with people in it on exhibit at the museum, they will most likely be clothed (picture Edward Hopper's depictions of everyday life). It would be challenging, however, to find a Renaissance painting *without* a nude or multiple nudes featured (picture Botticelli's *The Birth of Venus*). Popular during the fifteenth and sixteenth centuries, these paintings were not hidden for mature eyes to see, as their cinematic equivalents might be today; they were put on display in public places like halls of state and even churches. Go back even further in history and you'll find a more ubiquitous representation of the naked human form. Nearly all major non-portrait works from

Fig. 7. Nudity was commonplace in popular art in the Rennaissance, but aggresive sexual acts were not.

ancient Greece and Rome were nudes. It's evident throughout art history that there was no Nipplegate controversy in the time of Caesar.

While nudity in art was common up to a couple hundred years ago, there is very little evidence of popular art that depicted overtly sexual acts, not to mention violently sexual acts like those portrayed by Janet Jackson and Justin Timberlake in the 2004 Super Bowl halftime show. It appears that we have reversed the concept of common decency. In the Renaissance and before, the nude figure was something to be admired and appreciated, while sexual acts were hidden from public view. Today, we are inundated with sexual simulation throughout our popular culture, but nudity is strictly forbidden.

Interesting to note, however, is that the cultures involved all thought they were being modest. Nudes during the Renaissance were acceptable because they were depictions of ancient gods or fictitious characters like Venus. Only when the nudes were portrayed as everyday people (as in the Impressionist Édouard Manet's *Le déjeuner sur l'herbe* and *Olympia*) were they deemed controversial. Likewise, we have a very strict concept of decency today: there is to be no nudity in the public arena—outside of the rare nudist colonies, which are no doubt full of people no one really wants to see naked, anyway. In general, nudity is prohibited, which is why there was such uproar about the exposed breast in 2004.

Renaissance art and the Super Bowl halftime show

Fig. 8. Popular art became shocking when the nudes involved represented everyday people instead of gods or goddesses.

represent another monospective. Both cultural artifacts contain two distinct aspects: a concept of morality and the manifestations of that morality. Renaissance Europe and modern day America each believed that some things were morally acceptable while others were not, but the manifestations of that morality (nudity in the Renaissance and sexually aggressive dancing at the Super Bowl) were opposing. In essence, the two cultures agreed about morality, but the expression of that morality was different.

This dichotomy of belief systems based on a single innate tendency is also reflected in the concept of beauty throughout history. At the beginning of the last millennium, plump women were considered the most attractive of the species, an ideal that was recorded in the myriad paintings and sculptures that depicted the most beautiful women of the time. Today's society contrasts that mentality with an overwhelming attraction to thin women. Should we assume that we have changed the genetic urges that attract us to the fairer sex? Is our innate attraction so whimsical that it changes with the fashion of the day? Or, is there another reason why men used to like full-figured women hundreds of years ago but prefer thin women now? It turns out that our genes haven't changed—we're still sexually attracted to partners that would help to produce the best offspring. But our *information* has changed; a slightly rotund female used to imply wealth and healthy portions of food, whereas now the same characteristic implies less wealth and a healthy portion of McDonald's.

The dichotomy of beauty relates to the theory of concurrence in that, despite the seeming difference in standards of what is decent or attractive, we have and have always had a fairly strict sense of decency and beauty. In other words, we agree with our historic predecessors about the basics: modesty and healthfulness are good. The manifestations of these traits, however, are different from age to age and culture to culture, depending on the fashion and the media of the time.

But should we expect it to be any other way? Different cultures in different times require the population to show off their morality differently. When anthropologist H. H. Johnston reported on his visits to Central Africa in the 1890s, he told of ubiquitous nudity among the natives and very little clothing when it was worn. But surely this is due to the extreme heat that saturates the geographic area and the lack of appropriate textiles, not the lack of morals. In fact, as Johnston wrote, "It may sagely be asserted that the negro race in Central Africa is much more truly modest, is much more free from real vice than are most European nations."[23] This was true despite the accepted nudity, which was morally offensive to many Europeans at the time.

Modesty, then, is common to most examined cultures—even those that have very little need for clothing. The difference is in how that modesty is projected. Late nineteenth-century Central Africans and Renaissance painters displayed modesty through reserved behavior, whereas modern women display modesty by concealing their nipples. In each culture, modesty is valued, just not in the same way.

This cross-cultural agreement on the value of modesty is probably due to the deep social and psychological benefits we receive from it. As Havelock Ellis wrote in *Studies in the Psychology of Sex*, "It is necessary, before any psychology of sex can be arranged, to obtain a clear view of modesty."[24] In other words, a woman (because women control the pre-sex psychology of a couple) must display modesty to achieve sexual arousal and further emotions of love. Modesty, whether exhibited through fear of the sexual act or a sense of self-value, is one way to resist an attracted partner; and when attraction is resisted, it is usually exacerbated. Thus, as Charles Féré wrote in *The Evolution and Dissolution of the Sexual Instinct*, "The tendency to resist the male in most females is in reality nothing but a method of allurement."[25] The converse is also true. Ellis wrote that a woman lacking modesty also lacks "sexual attractiveness to the normal and average man."[26]

Believe it or not, even the raciest members of today's culture have a sense of modesty. Watching MTV or other media that depicts reckless youth rubbing their bodies against each other on the dance floor may make it hard to believe that these performers have any decorum, but they do. Girls on MTV may dance like strippers and make out with anyone who walks by, but they wouldn't dare reveal their nipples, an act that would violate their bizarre sense of modesty. Even when participants in this form of modesty break down once a year in the annual Mardi Gras celebration and unveil their breasts to wide-eyed drunken onlookers, the show is usually brief and limited. It's exceptionally rare for one of these exhibitionists to display absolutely no modesty and walk around completely naked the entire evening. If she were to do that, she would most likely receive looks of confusion rather than the looks of lust given to her flashing friends. Modesty exists in strip clubs, too. When a striptease takes place, the dancer usually starts off with at least some clothing or other barrier to complete nudity—the tease aspect—that is slowly shed throughout the performance.

Although it doesn't seem like it, we all share a sense of propriety that helps to facilitate attraction between the sexes. From the goddess in a Renaissance painting to a dancing college student in a typical MTV show, a sense of propriety exists in order to elicit attraction. The manifestations of our modesty are clearly different, but we all innately agree that modesty is a good thing.

right, left, and down the drain

Ask the typical American voter to define welfare, and he or she will usually say something like "financial assistance to the poor." A funny thing happens, however, somewhere in between the label "welfare" and its definition: it goes from being disliked to being the best thing since sliced bread in the mindset of the general public. According to one poll, Americans think we, as a nation, are spending *too much* on "welfare" (42 percent as opposed to 23 percent), but *too little* on "assistance to the poor" (68 percent to 7 percent).[27] To many, this seeming contradiction would be shocking, but as pollster Frank Luntz showed in his book *Words That Work*, it's not what you *say*, it's what they *hear* that matters. And what they hear with "welfare" is different from what they hear with "assistance to the poor."

But why is that? Why would the American populace have such a diametrically opposed view of what is basically the same thing? Luntz explains that, though people lump the two terms in the same category, "welfare" has a dramatically worse connotation than the generic but compassionate-sounding "assistance." This shows the trouble we face when we deal with language. Technically, welfare and assistance have the same definition, but they mean different things when applied in real life. Welfare has been associated with negative concepts like "welfare queen" and government handouts, while assistance to the poor doesn't have the same stigma.

Welfare means assistance, but the two labels conjure up completely different concepts, and this leads to a daunting task for communication and the goal of attaining universal concurrence. How can we possibly communicate when we are faced with such an oxymoronic mentality throughout society?

That was the question I hoped to answer in an online poll I conducted about the ever-touchy subject of political labels. The poll sought respondents' conceptions about political labels, specifically the terms "right-wing" and "left-wing." In the poll, respondents identified Hitler's Nazi Party as distinctly right-wing and the Stalinist Soviets as a distinctly left-wing party. Yet, when asked to describe either party, respondents described them as basically the same type of government. According to the respondents, *both* Nazis and Stalinists (1) controlled most of their country's economy and industry, (2) controlled most of their country's social freedoms, and (3) denied political freedoms, such as voting rights. In other words, 90 percent of the respondents pictured the Nazis and the Stalinist Soviets as the same type of government, but, shockingly, they also labeled them as opposites on the political spectrum.[28]

This is curious behavior to say the least. Why would nearly everyone in the poll indicate that the Nazis and Stalinists were identical in everything *except* for their political labels? Maybe there were other factors involved in the respondents' concepts of political wings? But in the same poll, respondents said that economic control (26 percent), human rights accordance (18 percent), and political freedoms (14 percent) were the most important factors in determining wing affiliation, which were the very aspects of a government found to be identical between the Nazis and Stalinists—solidifying the contradiction of terms.

Most historians have concurred that both regimes were brutal, racist, fiscally and socially oppressive, murderous, and socialist by name (the official Nazi party name, after all, was the National Socialist German Workers' Party). If they were so similar, why put the Nazis on the far right and the Stalinists on the far left?

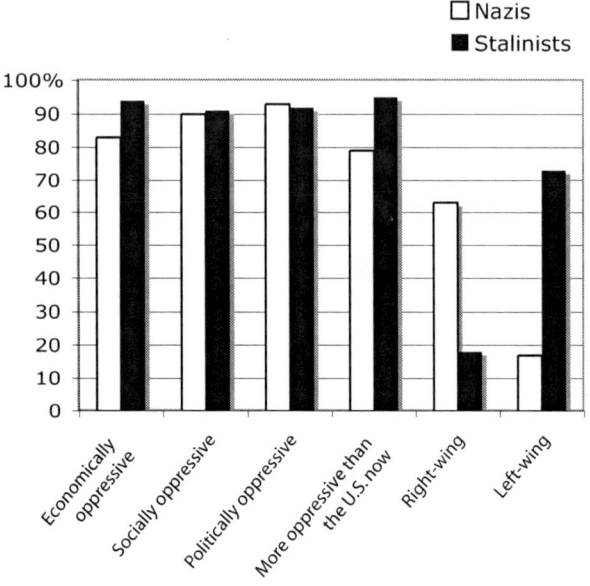

Fig. 9. Respondents labeled the Nazis and Stalinists identically except for their political wing.

Perhaps it would behoove us to follow the instructions from the first section of this book and define our terms. According to political historian Robert McHenry, the terms "left" and "right" were applied to the different sides of the National Assembly of France around the time of the French Revolution.[29] The Royalists (old guard) sat on the right and the anti-Royalists (new guard) sat on the left. This explains the modern connections between right/

left and conservative/radical dichotomies, but, unfortunately, it doesn't explain the confusion between the Nazis and Stalinists. The Nazis weren't right-wing with respect to conservatism—they were the new party, and they were radically altering the face of Germany with sweeping changes. Also, the Stalinists couldn't have been considered left-wing or radical because they had been maintaining the status quo since the revolution in 1917. It seems as though the general perception of these political wings is exactly backwards, at least in terms of the original intent.

Now the terms right- and left-wing are associated with Republicans and Democrats, and, though each party seems to be outgunning the other in an effort to spend as much of the taxpayer's money as possible, there are minor discrepancies between their ideologies. Generally, Republicans are in favor of more financial liberty (lower taxes), while the Democrats are in favor of more social liberty (same-sex marriage privileges). But both the Nazis and Stalinists restricted financial *and* social liberty, making the connection to modern day right- and left-wing parties obsolete.

It appears that we've gotten our labels all mixed up, but that isn't surprising in a political atmosphere that has more spin than a Maytag. Once a political label is identified with a party in the United States, it's tarred and feathered by the other side until it resembles a KFC accident. And, once the label is ugly enough, the side that's stuck with it attempts to dump it on the other team. This continues until the label is absolutely meaningless, as has been the case with terms like "right" and "left," but also "conservative," "liberal," and, as we saw above, "welfare." These terms have lost their original meaning and, in the process, they have become useless. As famed elocutionist C. S. Lewis noted, "When a word ceases to be a term of description and becomes merely a term of praise [or criticism], it no longer tells you facts about the object; it only tells you about the speaker's attitude to that object."[30] Right- and left-wing labels no longer speak to one's support of the current ruling power; they imply that one is a bad, amoral person who either wants poor people to suffer or wants everyone to become poor.

This degradation of terms matters because political pundits and the news media use labels like right- and left-wing as if these words mean something to their listeners and viewers. However, this may not always be the case. In a Harris Poll conducted in 2005, respondents revealed that about 50 percent of voters thought *conservatives* supported gun control and affirmative action—two positions that are usually vehemently opposed by self-professed conservatives.[31] The same poll showed that about 40 percent of respondents believed that *liberals* favored cutting taxes and opposed gun control measures—also both contradictory to self-proclaimed liberals. Social scientist Leo Bogart thinks that such contradictions in political labels arise from inappropriate use of the terms. As he explains, "The confusion over what the widely used political labels actually mean reflects their common use as epithets rather than as true descriptions of people's beliefs."

Regardless of the confusion of labels, political partisans continue to get worked up about their self-conceived moral dualism, and they think they're fighting the good fight by opposing the other wing. Unfortunately, when we lose sight of the true definitions of words and instead concentrate on arbitrary name-calling, there *is* no good fight, and everyone loses. As the red and blue states concentrate on fighting with each other, the entire country is slowly moving away from its original colorless intent. Just as poll respondents placed the Nazis and Stalinists on the right and left wings, respectively, even though these parties were seen as practically identical, voters in the U.S. have placed Republicans and Democrats on opposite sides of the political spectrum, as well, though they are, in most respects, the same beast. To paraphrase a quote by John Kenneth Galbraith, under a right-wing government, man exploits man; under a left-wing government, it's just the opposite; either way, the people lose.[32]

Ron Paul, in his modern-day political manifesto *Revolution*, pointed out that Republicans and Democrats posture their views as opposing, but, in the end, these views amount to the same thing. Paul reported on a supposed anti-government-waste Republican who condemned pork-barrel spending and denounced $10 million in frivolous outlays only to ignore the other $2.917 trillion dollars being spent each year.[33] He also showed that supposed anti-war Democrats have continuously voted for the Iraq war, while also maintaining their own pet military interventions.

My point here is not to say that either party is right or wrong, but rather to show that modern politics uses the moral dualistic vocabulary of right and left wings to create an artificial perception of two entities which are really the same thing. Voters today suffer from a monospective as two labels (right and left) are applied to one concept (more government), and the subsequent confusion allows the entire situation to deteriorate. Ronald Reagan explained it best in a debate when he said, "You and I are told we must choose between a left or right, but I suggest there is no such thing as a left or right. There is only an up or down. Up to man's age-old dream—the maximum of individual freedom consistent with order—or down to the ant heap of totalitarianism."[34] The problem in today's society is not the left or the right; it's partisanship itself. People assume that everything associated with the *other* party is wrong or evil, and they give everything associated with *their* party or wing a pass. When this happens, truth suffers.

It may sound counterintuitive, but it's clear to me that people who vote Democratic and those who vote Republican all want the same things. Both sides want safety from foreign military threats and protection from criminals. Both Republicans and Democrats want better education for the country's children. Both want affordable healthcare and more jobs for working Americans. All of these things boil down to one common goal: liberty. It just so happens that Democrats tend to work toward greater social liberties, while Republicans generally work for more economic liberties. Democrats don't want to punish the wealthy and give handouts to freeloaders, though; they just want everyone to be able to live their own lives free of government intrusion, and they want poorer people to experience the good life, just as the wealthy do. Likewise, Republicans don't want the poor to suffer or the minority social groups to be persecuted; they want everyone to be able to reap what they sew, and they want the majority population to have the same benefits as everyone else.

Though not immediately evident to arguing Republicans and Democrats, there is an efficient path to all of these goals, and we would all agree on that path if only we knew what it was. Agreement can't happen, though, when we apply political labels to potential paths to liberty, saying, "This is a Democratic idea," or "This is a Republican idea." If an idea becomes a partisan idea, it immediately gains support from one third of the population and vehement opposition from another third. If you identify yourself with a specific political party, disagreeing with that party on any issue is tantamount to treason. The more you identify yourself with a label, the more you must defend anything associated with that label as a matter of consistency and self-preservation. This idea, which I will develop further in Book II of *Everyone Agrees*, is one of the main reasons why disagreements arise and why we maintain so much divisiveness between members of a society that generally wants the same thing.

It's also why politics is a taboo subject of discussion at work or at a social event. One moment, Bobby and Sally from accounting may be enjoying a witty conversation about the latest *American Idol* winner while they sample the veggie platter and cheese dip; the next minute, they're bitter enemies when it becomes apparent that Bobby is a Democrat and Sally is a Republican. No longer are Bobby's comments about *American Idol*'s television network, Fox, benign—all of a sudden, they're snide remarks about a company that supports George W. Bush. And no longer are Sally's remarks about the vegetables innocuous—now, they're pointed attacks on the illegal immigrants who harvested them. A convivial conversation between two rational people can be ruined when politics comes into the forum.

That's why, when someone at a party asks me which political party I support, I like to answer, "I'm with the party that supports liberty." If the person asking is like most people, he or she will reply, "Me, too." Sometimes, however, I receive the reply, "Well, which party is that?" This person is looking for a label—he isn't concerned with the concept of liberty; he is interested in political teams and whether I can be attacked on those terms. If one maintains the loftier goals of government rather than the partisan particulars, there seems to be a lot more agreement.

If we do not remove political epithets from our vocabulary, we risk losing our language altogether. We will be forced to choose politicians that stand for a label and not a genuine idea (some readers may think this is already the case). Meaningless political labels do nothing but perpetuate the moral dualism that infests our system and leads us away from the truth. Unless we can avoid the artificial division that's created by the political monospective, universal concurrence will remain just another pipe dream.

communication breakdown

With the ambiguity we face in using labels, especially political labels, universal concurrence seems like a daunting task. Luckily, we find help in the form of an innate urge to agree. While agreement in the political sphere seems unattainable, agreement in everyday life seems easily accessible—almost unavoidable. In fact, concurrence is so persistent that it shows up in places we would never imagine.

Thomas Schelling, an American economist famous for his war games throughout the Cold War, revealed in the 1960s that people tend to agree on certain things even without communication. In a heavily-cited study, Schelling asked the following hypothetical question to college students in New Haven, Connecticut: if you were supposed to meet someone in New York City tomorrow, but didn't know where, where would you go to meet them? Surprisingly, the majority of students chose the information desk at Grand Central Station.[35] Furthermore, nearly all of the students independently chose noon as the meeting time. While not everyone chose Grand Central Station, the fact that the majority of students agreed on a meeting place in a city as large and diverse as New York without communication is remarkable.

Schelling attributed this amazing behavior to a universal urge to emphasize particular focal points in any given situation. We identify the particular focus naturally, so we don't need to communicate it in order to arrive at the same conclusion as others who are trying to do the same thing. For instance, if two people were looking at a piece of paper with three blue squares and one red square printed on it and were asked to select the same square independently in order to receive a prize, the participants would naturally pick the lone red square because of its novelty.

Focal points like these exist outside of economics classes, too. For instance, when many people want to do the same thing at the same time (like sit down to eat or ride an amusement park ride), the natural focal point is first-come, first-served (FCFS). Without knowing the time constraints of everyone involved, the most obvious way to determine who gets to go first is to determine who showed up first. Recently, several grocery stores have made an effort to promote the FCFS standard. Whole Foods, the gourmet natural foods store based in California, changed from a multiple-line checkout system to a single-line system in its New York locations in order to take advantage of FCFS. The response has been positive for the grocery chain. A single line that branches off to multiple registers and regularly stacks up to over fifty people can be traversed in under four minutes compared to a shorter line dedicated to just one register.[36] Because it eliminates the risk of getting in the "slow line" behind the troubled customer with 9,000 coupons and a slow check-writing style, the single line is more equitable and adheres to the focal point of FCFS.

Focal points like the red square in the coordination game and first-come, first-served at the grocery store are called Schelling points, and they reveal an interesting aspect of concurrence: we don't have to tell each other what we believe in order to come to the same conclusion; in some situations, we intuitively agree. In the four squares game, one square is prominent, so two people can agree on it naturally without prior communication. This is an extremely simplified coordination game; even if all the squares were the same color (i.e., there was no focal point), the players would still have a 25% chance of picking the same square if choosing at random. Similarly, FCFS is fairly obvious since it maintains the status of its participants. What if the options for focal points were unlimited? Do these natural places of agreement still occur if the choices are completely up to the participant?

That's what I hoped to find out when I asked people to picture a scene—you may want to play along by imagining it yourself. I asked respondents to imagine someone driving a sports car in the middle of the day. While I made sure to leave several important aspects of the scene ambiguous, most participants imagined the exact same scene. Three out of four people envisioned a red sports car, and the same number pictured the sports car as a convertible.[37] Even a third of the respondents agreed on the location of the car: a winding coastal road. The respondents didn't agree on everything in their imagined scenes (the driver's sex was pictured as male and as having brown hair slightly more often than other options), but most respondents at least equated "red" and "convertible" with "sports car."

People even tend to agree on one of the most complex aspects of life: human behavior. One study asked participants to judge a stranger's behavior based on character traits like talkativeness, humor, and intelligence. The results showed that a vast majority of people agree on traits about strangers. Out of the 100 traits measured, the participants agreed significantly on 85.[38] In other words, if someone sees a stranger as a neurotic, self-defensive chatterbox, there's a good chance that everyone else will agree about that. A later study then asked people to use those assessed personality traits to predict behavior.[39] For example, I bet that neurotic, self-defensive chatterbox is going to start telling me about the latest conspiracy theory pretty soon. The results showed that people can actually predict what others will do based on their personality assessments—an amazing feat. As psychologist David Funder, who conducted the studies, said, "No computerized assessment, actuarial prediction, or other artificial system has this ability; the ordinary human judge outperforms them all."

Given these studies and Schelling's work, it seems that people agree just fine without communicating; but when they start to communicate, agreement becomes a bit more difficult. Would it be reasonable, then, to conclude that communication itself is a deterrent to agreement? A study conducted in 1987 gives credence to this idea. Psychologist Paul Andreassen separated MIT students into two groups of mock stock traders. One group of students traded familiar stocks and only received information on whether their stocks were trading up or down. The other group was given the up- and down-ticks of their stocks, as well, but they were also given a stream of news that provided reasons for the stocks' performance. Andreassen was surprised to find that the traders who had to rely on just the up- and down-ticks of their stocks fared better than the traders who had access to the explanatory news like that seen on Yahoo! Finance or CNBC (e.g., "Stocks Fall on Rising Oil, Unease About Financials").[40] In other words, more information was not beneficial for those particular traders.

Andreassen's study seemed to indicate that more information is bad for decision-making. But that doesn't quite explain the situation—it's not that more information is bad, it's that information needs to be applied appropriately to be effective. Andreassen's subjects didn't apply the news appropriately—they overreacted to it, giving it more weight than was necessary or thinking about how other stockholders would react to it instead of looking at the performance of the stock itself. In another study conducted at the University of Colorado, mock investors reacted irrationally to news about potential investments in another way. The study revealed that information about an investment had a distinctively high impact on the investor's decision-making process, but only if that information was presented in "story order."[41] In other words, people reacted differently to the same information if it was presented as a narrative.

This, of course, happens every day in real markets. Investors receive limited information and overreact to it, thinking that others will act on the same information in the same way. This speculation usually results in a financial bubble, which is an irrational inflation of an equity's price. And, as we've seen in the case of Internet stocks just after the year 2000 and the housing market after 2006, financial bubbles have a nasty habit of blowing up and causing a lot of financial pain. However, information isn't the problem; overreaction to it is. If the information available to investors was used appropriately, we could avoid bubbles and their unpleasant successors.

Similarly, communication is not the problem when it comes to politics or other touchy topics; it's what we do with communication that fouls up the situation. Ask any therapist or counselor to name the main problem in relationships, and he or she will say that the inability to communicate is usually at fault. Thus, more information is good, as long as it is used appropriately.

In Schelling's meet-a-stranger game mentioned above, the point was to agree; but the point in politics these days seems to be disagreement. After all, if your party is out of power yet you profess the same ideals as the party in power, you have nothing new or different to offer, and you will most certainly lose the election. And when we humans *want* to disagree, we find very creative ways to make conflict happen. We associate ourselves with the right or left wing, doing everything in our power to degrade the other side. We associate that other side and its labels with bad characteristics and take all the good attributes for our side. As shown above, this just increases divisive moral dualism and reduces the value of the labels we use in discussion.

onward

We can start moving toward unity by overlooking labels and focusing on their meaning instead. While this skill may be out of use in a vehemently dualistic society, it's not completely lost. A popular email forward demonstrates the ability of our brains to get to the point of a message even if the message is imperfect. If you can uesdnatnrd waht yu'roe rdaneig ni tihs esntecen, yrou'e orevcmongi a onomspcetiv adn hleipgn faclitieat cmonmcautoni. The common explanation for this phenomenon is that, when reading, we naturally look at the entire word and not the exact location of the letters in each word. We can grasp the meaning of a word and a sentence even if they aren't perfectly formed (but don't tell my editor that). This shows that when we want to understand, our brains are very effective in making that happen.

Our subconscious minds are working just as hard in face-to-face conversation, too. Studies have shown that when people communicate in person, they use gestures and movements that seem almost dance-like. From a slight turn of the head to a gesture with one's hand, little physical movements communicate in a conversation as much or more than the actual words used. What's more is that the listener in a conversation reacts to verbal cues from the speaker within 1/48th to 1/24th of a second, making the verbal-physical dance most certainly subconscious.[42] This conversational dance promotes discussion between speaker and listener and helps to facilitate understanding.

With such strong forces on the side of communication, it's hard to believe that misunderstandings happen so often. But as we saw above, the discrepancy between labels and their meanings rears its ugly head more often than we'd like. In this case, people have the same idea but use different labels for it, resulting in a monospective disagreement. Adherents from different religions and even atheists experience the same sensations but label their experience differently, leading to confusion and sometimes antagonism. In addition, people oppose each other's core beliefs, such as morality, when in fact their core beliefs are the same; it's the superficial manifestations of those core beliefs that differ. For example, the bare-breasted Central-African girl may be just as modest as the fully-clothed Victorian lady despite the outward display of each. The monospective shows up in politics most dramatically. People assume that the right and left wings of the political spectrum are opposites because the words "right" and "left" also represent opposite directions, but the labels are basically meaningless and lead to an artificial divide that usually impedes progress.

Much of the animosity between warring factions can be avoided if we choose to look at the true intentions behind the labels we use. Religious adherents and atheists should consider the similarities between God and the numinous, just as right- and left-wingers should consider the possibility that their vehement opposition might be artificial. Instead of focusing on the exactness of the labels used in a discussion, it behooves us to look to the meaning behind them. William Shakespeare brought eloquence to this subject through his character Juliet in a timeless soliloquy:

> *'Tis but thy name that is my enemy;*
> *Thou art thyself, though not a Montague.*
> *What's Montague? it is nor hand, nor foot,*
> *Nor arm, nor face, nor any other part*
> *Belonging to a man. O, be some other name!*
> *What's in a name? that which we call a rose*
> *By any other name would smell as sweet;*
> *So Romeo would, were he not Romeo call'd,*
> *Retain that dear perfection which he owes*
> *Without that title. Romeo, doff thy name,*
> *And for that name which is no part of thee*
> *Take all myself.*[43]

Thanks, Bill. I couldn't have said it better myself.

part III

science, socrates, and sense

In George Bernard Shaw's play, *Saint Joan*, Joan d'Arc describes to a skeptical audience how she receives instructions supernaturally. Joan says, "I hear voices telling me what to do. They come from God."

The skeptic disagrees and says no, "They come from your *imagination*."

"Of course," Joan replies. "That is *how* the messages of God come to us."[1]

The scene masterfully depicts a monospective as described in the last part and shows how people can really agree without being aware of it. Joan is the native Hawaiian using the term "Mauna Kea," and the skeptic is the missionary using the term "White Mountain." They're talking about the same thing while using different words. Both these monospectives and the dispectives from Part I show how people actually agree—even when they think they don't.

Assumptions in human discourse concerning dispectives and monospectives can cause communication problems (e.g., the atheist/believer disagreement about an undefined "God" or the artificial right/left political divide). But is it possible to overcome these problems? Can we avoid dispectives and monospectives and come to understand a universal perspective—a *panspective*? I believe so. If the Hiloan and the Puako native with different perspectives of Mauna Kea were each to simply take a trip around the mountain to see the other side (or hop on Google Maps to see an aerial view of the island), they would surely come to mutual agreement on the towering mound. Similarly, if the missionary and the native Hawaiian would simply explain what their labels represent, they would also come to the same conclusions. As Joan d'Arc and the skeptic in Shaw's play found out, we can perceive the entire mountain of truth through explanation and discourse.

Our first task in attempting to gain a universal perspective, at least with respect to human morality, is to figure out if one actually exists. To do so, we will need to look into the moral relativity that pervades modern discourse today. Many popular books released in the last few years purport that we humans behave in irrational ways and that we can't control our irrational behavior. And if we have no choice in how we behave, the idea of right and wrong goes out the window. These authors are promoting a scientific-sounding, logical moral relativism, but we will see that what they purport is illogical and they actually contradict themselves. Not only do we act rationally and participate in moral decision-making, but the same moral relativists who deny that fact actually prove themselves wrong in the end.

Next, we will establish the presence of a universal truth in morality—something that we can all agree on—and examine the tools that point to a panspective. Physicists, including great thinkers like Newton and Einstein, are constantly progressing toward a unified theory in their field that is simple yet can explain all known mechanical phenomena. We will see how this concept of a unified theory can be applied to morality so as to easily explain the right and wrong in every situation.

Until scientists discover that unified theory, they are forced to make partial theories—judgments—based on their experimental findings (e.g., the theory of relativity, the uncertainty principle). While these judgments aren't the entire truth, they are accurate aspects of the entire truth. Scientists and laymen accept these judgments and look forward to each new one that is presented. When it comes to morality, however, judgment isn't as highly esteemed; we're told not to judge, but rather to ask ourselves, "Who am I to judge?" But just as scientists make judgments that don't explain the entire truth, so can we non-scientists make judgments in everyday life, whether moral or not. We'll see how judgment is not only inevitable but also positive, and how the moral judge must have an open mind in order for a moral judgment to hold any validity. Then, we'll visit a third-grade classroom to see how an ancient Athenian is still impacting the minds of youngsters. By asking questions to arrive at a shared understanding, the Socratic method helps us acknowledge the existence of a universal panspective on which everyone can agree.

The ancient inhabitants of the big island of Hawaii used to believe that heaven existed at the top of Mauna Kea, and that the gods and goddesses lived there—and it's no wonder why. The summit of Mauna Kea has been described as a pinnacle of rocks from which you can view one of the most amazing scenes on

Earth, a 360-degree view of the clouds, islands, ocean, and sky that's beyond words and pictures. Can you imagine a more valuable reason to ascend a mountain—to gain perspective on not just the mountain itself, but on everything around it in an experience that transcends words? That would be, as the Hawaiians claimed precisely, just like heaven.

relatively speaking

If the early twentieth century can be thought of as the age of popular psychology with the likes of Sigmund Freud making headlines, the young twenty-first century can be thought of as the era in which we moved backwards in the science of the mind. Recent pop-psychology books like *Predictably Irrational* by Dan Ariely, *Fooled by Randomness* by Nassim Taleb, and *Sway* by Ori and Rom Brafmanall provide entertaining accounts of how we humans do some things that just don't make sense. One book describes the way in which we tend to buy things just because they have a "for sale" sign on them and not because the price is right. Another book shows how we order drinks at a restaurant based on what others ordered before us, not on what we think will taste good. Yet another text details how we gamble, are racist, and smoke cigarettes even though we know that these things are bad for us and for society. The authors of the above books make a clear and convincing argument that we humans are just slaves to randomness—that we have no control over our erratic behavior—and the general public continues to buy that idea wholesale.

The idea that we are irrational beyond our control and that we can only hope to acknowledge our random actions is peculiarly reminiscent of the ideology that was prevalent before the Enlightenment. In medieval times, it was common for people to believe that nature was random and completely irrational. If reasons were given to inexplicable acts, they were based on whimsical supernatural beings: Bartholemew's house burnt down because he must have angered God; Ezekiel caught the plague because of the devil; and Mathilda smelled so bad because she was possessed by demons. Oh, that poor wretched Mathilda! But while those in the medieval ages were only trying to give a cause to seemingly irrational behavior, their opinions were nothing more than names applied to mysterious events. For instance, medieval physicians explained their patients' ailments with a description of the four humors. If Mathilda became angry, she was highly *choleric* and had an imbalance of yellow bile.

Science changed all that, first by proving that different levels of yellow fluid in the blood don't affect emotion and then by finding the real cause for anger—in this case, living in a time in which there were so many pseudoscientists. With science, what was once unknowable became common sense; what was once confusing became clear; and what once seemed irrational became the logical actions of a mechanical universe. With the dawn of science, fact was born.

But fact, especially in the realm of psychology, has had a tumultuous journey since its inception, and along the way it has confronted skeptics, unbelievers, and more pseudoscience. The obstacles to understanding human behavior were varied and diverse, but they usually ended up resulting in the development of fields like phrenology, a pseudoscience in which a patient's personality and intelligence are determined by the bumps and fissures on his or her head. To me, phrenology seems more like an excuse to elicit head massages ("Ooh, yeah, can you rub a little more on my *extroversion bump?*"), but the practitioners of the pseudoscience claimed to actually be able to assess personality traits from the shape of the skull. As with most pseudoscience, the basis of phrenology was valid to some extent, as it has been well established that certain regions of the brain (not the skull) are associated with specific behaviors and areas of knowledge, but the head-massagers didn't quite hit the nail on its head.

At the end of the nineteenth century, the science of human behavior moved from phrenology to less speculative fields. Freud contributed a scientific approach to human behavior with psychoanalysis, which consisted of an investigation of the mind (conscious and subconscious) and therapy using that investigation.[2] Freud also brought the science of the mind to public awareness. His theories influenced much of the popular art of the day, including Alfred Hitchcock's thriller films (*Spellbound*'s central characters were psychoanalysts, for example).[3]

Recently, technology has helped to move the science of the mind away from psychoanalysis toward a more mechanical, predictable science; and, as science has advanced, so, too, has our understanding of our own behavior. Brain scanners and other neuroscience-affiliated devices have helped sociologists and psychologists actually see into the working brain and gain insight into why we do the things we do. Researchers using a driving simulator in one study were able to predict about 95 percent of test subjects' responses based on seemingly unrelated preparatory behavior.[4] For example, when subjects were instructed to change lanes, they predictably initiated the act by centering the car in their current lane.

In addition, the gambling study described in the last part

revealed something further using brain-imaging technology. In the study, subjects had to choose between gambling for $100 and simply taking home $40. When the take-home amount was described as *losing* $60 (from the original $100), subjects were much more willing to gamble than when the same option was described as *keeping* $40. Using fMRI technology, researchers found that the word "lose" triggered a much stronger response in brain regions involved with emotion than did the word "keep."[5] It turns out that we have a much greater fear of losing a certain amount than keeping that same amount. The behavior wasn't irrational; it just involved more than met the eye.

Despite our scientific advancements, some people, like the authors of the irrationality books noted above, maintain that, much of the time, we are just not logical and there's no way to explain some of the things we do—like buying a sofa because it's marked with a "for sale" sign, not because it's a good deal. And, while most of what these authors assert is harmless ambivalence toward our confusing behavior, some of their claims are not so benign. One implication drawn from the authors is that government needs to control us more because we cannot control ourselves. Dan Ariely, author of *Predictably Irrational*, wrote that if you agree with the points he's making in his book, then "government must play a larger role in regulating some market activities, even if this limits free enterprise."[6]

Another implication is that, since we have no control over our behavior, there is no objective right or wrong in our actions. If we can't control our irrational minds, we can't be blamed for our vices, the authors claim. This train of thought is a precursor to the moral relativism mentioned in the introduction, a philosophy that claims that there is no objective right or wrong, just relative morality based on a given group, society, or country. The philosophy is certainly logical; after all, if we really can't help ourselves from doing irrational acts, how can those acts be considered wrong? With irrational minds, morality becomes a subjective, personal endeavor that has no meaning when applied to other people or groups. Fuel is added to this philosophical flame when one considers the title (if not the content) of Einstein's groundbreaking work, the theory of relativity, which inadvertently implies that nature itself is relative.

To be sure, our minds work relatively. We perceive things based on our environment, not on absolutes. When I turn on my car in the quiet morning to a blaring radio, I'm shocked into turning the volume down; yet I was comfortable with the same volume level just twelve hours before when the radio was competing with noises from the interstate. The spa outside feels scorching hot when I've been resting in sixty-degree temperatures, but lukewarm after exercising in ninety-degree heat. Some bread can taste sweet after a short fast, but would be flavorless after eating a doughnut.

Context is an extremely important element of perception, and this includes our perception of morality. For example, we give Thomas Jefferson a pass for owning slaves because he grew up in a climate that basically required him to do so and then helped to forge the ideology that later freed *all* of the slaves in the United States. We also pardon Miep Gies for lying to the Gestapo while helping to hide Anne Frank and her family during World War II. In the less important realm of celebrities, we accept the delinquencies of bizarre, child-negligent celebrities like Britney Spears because, as the popular magazines make clear, they're just human, too. Additionally, each one of us only has access to our own perspective, making our decisions and morality good relative only to us.

Thus, morality has to be relative, right? To put it succinctly, the answer is no. Moral relativism is based on the lack of control that we have over our irrational behavior, but what the irrationality-promoters failed to point out while describing this irrational behavior is that it's not really irrational after all. For example, consumers need some sort of reference to determine the value of an item, so we use what behavioral economists call an anchor as the basis of our decision to buy that item. Most of us don't know whether that bottle of 2003 Chateauneuf du Pape is worth the $99.99 sale price, but we at least know that $99.99 is a better deal than the regular price of $139, so we're more likely to buy the bottle on sale. In addition, because we value originality in our society almost as much as we value a tasty beverage, we order a beer that no one else in our dinner party has ordered even if it doesn't appeal to us as much as another drink, presumably so that the group is smarter as a whole when it has collectively experienced more. And we gamble, are racist, and smoke because doing so satisfies various instincts, including greed, protection, and self-identity, despite what the behavior does to our common sense and personal health. In other words, there *are* rational reasons for the seemingly irrational behavior we exhibit—the books mentioned above would be a lot shorter and much more boring otherwise. While not really admitting that our decisions are rational, the irrationality writers actually do explain *why* we do the irrational-seeming things that we do. And, once there's a reason for the behavior, logic returns to the equation—we're not irrational; it just seems that way.

Rational behavior means we actually have a choice in what we do. We can choose our personal pleasure over the good of a neighbor; we can decide to help others or to cause harm; and we can do right or wrong. And, despite what we choose to do, there is an objective morality in each situation. Just as the blaring radio has the same volume on a quiet morning and a noisy afternoon, the spa is a constant 104 degrees whether you're cold or hot yourself, and the bread always has the same number of calories, the moral law is constant, too. Our perception of any given situation may change, but the morality involved does not. So, unfortunately for Thomas Jefferson, Miep Gies, and Britney Spears, it's not okay to own slaves, lie, or be negligent, no matter what the circumstances.

The skeptical reader may ask, what if someone has a mental disorder and can't control his or her bad behavior? If this was the case and a certain illness took away an individual's power of free will, then that person alone could be labeled irrational, and proper measures should be taken to prevent harm from being done. But learning that a mental illness leads to a specific antisocial behavior doesn't make the behavior acceptable; it just explains why it happened.

Truth isn't restricted to one person or one group; it exists outside of limited experience. Just as the authors above failed to see the contradiction in explaining the *causes* of *irrational* behavior (irrational behavior doesn't have causes), moral relativists fail to see the contradiction in applying their lack of a universal morality universally. If something is wrong, it is always wrong. Consistency is the key to universal morality, and, as we will see, it's the central concept of this book. But before I can describe a universal morality, I must make it clear that one exists; to do so, I'd like to enlist the help of two brilliant people with big hair.

weird science

If Isaac Newton had been alive in 1905 when Einstein released his special theory of relativity, which antiquated Newton's theories, he probably would have bought the young physicist a beer at the local pub and then begun to wonder why he was the only one still wearing a gigantic powdered wig. I don't think the brilliant mathematician and mechanic would have snickered and sneered at the thought of being proven wrong after having put so much time and effort into his theories. And Newton probably wouldn't have been sad when Einstein overturned his theory; to the contrary, he most likely would have been fascinated. This is because science does not follow the dualistic "you're wrong, I'm right" view described in the introduction. Nor does it adhere to the relativistic view that there is no right or wrong. Science follows the third way—the way of concurrence.

Scientists like Newton aren't simply better at hiding their pride than people without huge wigs; it's just that the nature of their industry lends itself to constant revision. The typical scientist knows that his or her discoveries aren't the entire truth; they're just steps toward the truth. As theoretical physicist Brian Greene wrote of past scientific discoveries in *The Fabric of the Cosmos*, each scientific discovery "contribute[d] its own piece to the puzzle, even though no one knew—and we still don't know—what grand synthesizing picture comprises all the puzzle's pieces."[7] So, despite each scientist's inability to explain *everything* with his or her discovery or theory, it's clear that his or her discovery helps us to inch closer to realizing an overarching, ultimate truth.

While each scientific discovery trumps those that precede it, that doesn't necessarily mean that the previous theories were erroneous. When Einstein came up with relativity, he didn't say Newton was *wrong* for believing space and time were static; as Greene wrote, that would be a naïve assumption. From Newton's point of view, which is the same as our everyday experience, those theories are extremely accurate. Likewise, in Einstein's frame of reference (from the point of view of extremely fast-moving and extremely massive objects), the German genius's theories are extremely accurate.

But if scientific theories aren't wrong, just accurate in their own framework, this starts to sound suspiciously like a scientific rendition of the moral relativism I finished discrediting. The relativist would argue that Newton was right in his realm and Einstein right in his, but that neither scientist can claim that the theory of the other is wrong. And if there is no wrong, there is no right, right? Moreover, many even see Einstein's theory of relativity as the scientific proof that opened the door to much of the moral relativism in the twentieth century. As Walter Isaacson wrote in *Time*'s "Person of the Century" article about Einstein, "Indirectly, relativity paved the way for a new relativism in morality, arts and politics."[8]

But while Einstein couldn't claim that Newton was *wrong*, per se, he could claim that the scientific relativist was. There is truth in the universe, and there is a right in science. In addition, we can grasp it. As Donald Simanek of Lock Haven University put it in his Glossary of Frequently Misused and Misunderstood Physics Terms and Concepts, "Special relativity shows that only certain measurable things are relative, but in a precisely and mathematically specific way, and other things are, not relative, for all observers agree on them."[9] Einstein himself made it a point to reject the relativism that sprung artificially from his theory by saying, "The most incomprehensible thing about the world is that it is comprehensible."[10]

Instead of a form of dualism or relativism, science employs a third mentality—one that mirrors the central theme of this book. Newton's theories were *right*, just not in all situations, including the high-gravity and high-speed ones that Einstein was considering. In fact, they were both right. Einstein didn't contradict Newton's theories; he simply improved them and opened them up to a wider framework. Newton and Einstein agree; the only thing that separates them is Einstein's added perspective. Newton was describing his side of Mauna Kea in his age and by the time Einstein had described his perspective, he had moved up the mountain to gain a wider perspective. In this respect, science is a constant progression toward a unified perspective (the peak of Mauna Kea) and an ultimate truth—a goal that at least science seems to be capable of achieving. As Greene wrote, "The pattern traced out during the last three hundred years of discovery gives tantalizing evidence that such a [unifying] theory can be developed."[11]

Can we apply the same goal of unifying truth in science to something a little less precise, like morality? I think we can, but to do so, I'll need to clear up some ideas that have been muddied by decades of moral smog.

judgment day

"Who am I to judge?" the humble-sounding person asks. The question seems harmless enough, but it usually serves the exact opposite of its intended goal. When someone asks that rhetorical question, he is basically implying that he *shouldn't* judge someone else. Moreover, someone who says "Who am I to judge?" usually means to imply that *no one* should judge in that situation, otherwise, there wouldn't be a reason to ask their rhetorical question aloud. But isn't that in itself a judgment? Unfortunately for the person who wishes to seem nonjudgmental, the answer is yes. What most self-professed nonjudgmental people fail to realize is that their plea for a judgment-free world is, in fact, a judgment itself.

Contrary to what pseudo-nonjudgmental people profess, judging is not the rude and offensive act that some people make it out to be. As we'll see, judging is unavoidable and it's also good. But for a judgment to be worth anything at all, the judge must have an open mind, as well. In the end, it's close-mindedness that's the sin, not judgment.

We all judge and we do it constantly. From opinions ("That new dress from Anthropologie looks hot on you") to predictions ("This county is going down the toilet if what's-his-face is elected") to rhetorical questions ("How great was that new Pixar movie?!") we make judgments all the time. In fact, we can barely open our mouths without passing judgment, which means that pretty much everything we say follows the definition of a judgment—a reasonable conclusion about a given topic. If we didn't judge at all, we'd be a very quiet species. Judgment is simply a summary of our beliefs and experiences, and, in this respect, judging is good.

Some people, however, have deemed certain judgments unacceptable. Your friend Sally might like your judgment when you compliment her on her haircut, but when you tell her that smoking cigars in the office isn't good for anyone, she'll tell you to mind your own business—and she'll add that it's wrong to judge. She might even evoke Jesus, who challenged those who were ready to stone an alleged criminal with the command, "He that is without sin among you, let him first cast a stone at her."[12] People shouldn't attack, ridicule, or, for heaven's sake, throw stones at someone for mistakes they've made themselves; but, beyond condemning brutal physical abuse, Jesus wasn't condemning all judgment—he was condemning hypocrisy (as well as saving a poor lady from a horrible and unnecessary beating). To say that it is wrong to judge is a judgment in itself; as such, it creates a contradiction.

We should judge, partly because doing so is unavoidable—you can't get up in the morning without *judging* that getting up will be worthwhile—but also partly because judgment helps us to grow. Each judgment we make, even though it's not a statement of complete truth or enlightenment, inches us closer to that truth, working in much the same way as scientific judgments do. A judgment is a summary of what we know regarding a particular subject, and it helps us to package a potentially messy concept into one statement and then build from that summary.

Not surprisingly, I've judged that it is okay to judge, but there are qualifications. For a judgment to have any validity, one must have an open mind. The judgment that Porsches are the most fun cars to drive means very little if the person making such a judgment won't drive a Mazda. One's endorsement of John McCain for president doesn't carry much weight if he or she refuses to listen to Barack Obama. And an atheist or a believer spouts empty claims unless he or she has truly listened to the other side.

To many, an open-minded judgment may seem like a contradiction. How can someone judge another, but still be unbiased? Or, how can one have an open mind *and* an open mouth? The friction between the two ideas is understandable and common, but it's based on a misnomer about the concept of open-mindedness. Many think that to have an open mind, one must *accept* everything about everyone else, similar to the moral relativism described above. However, that's not what open-mindedness truly is. To have an open mind, you don't have to accept everything; you just have to be *open* to accepting everything. In other words, you just have to be open to listening and comparing novel ideas. Open-minded people take in and genuinely process all pertinent information, excluding nothing without a fair assessment. When discussing the merits of a presidency, the best NFL quarterback, or who should get the last piece of blackberry pie, all participants need to take into account all information regarding the president, the quarterback, or the slice of berry goodness. The participants involved may not change their positions due to the new information they receive (though it's highly unlikely that new information wouldn't alter one's perspective at all), but, for their judgment to matter, they must be open to everything.

But if everyone was open to all information, shouldn't they all come to the same conclusion that Bush was a sub-par president, Peyton Manning is the best quarterback ever, and the philosopher should get the last slice of pie? Yes—and a universal perspective is the goal of concurrence. But a consensus will occur only if—and this is a big "if"—all information is presented to everyone in the same way. As described in the first part, a consensus is guaranteed only if two perspectives align perfectly. Otherwise, two debaters are applying one label to two different ideas and there is room for incongruity and disagreement.

Luckily, we don't need to have identical perspectives,

backgrounds, or histories to agree; we can arrive at identical perspectives—a universal perspective—through discourse and explanation. All we need to facilitate an explanation is an open mind and a desire to seek the truth. So, if you're still open, I'd like to tackle another concept that has been muddled by moral relativism: the idea that everything can be judged right or wrong.

it takes guts

The popular television show *Heroes* is unique in its science-fiction genre partly because it's not clear whether its characters are good or bad—they're morally ambiguous. This ambiguity is present in most of the characters, but it's blatantly evident in Niki, whose alter ego, Jessica, shows up in Niki's mirror reflection and takes over when Niki blacks out. Niki is a single mom just trying to support her son, but her alter ego is a ferocious criminal capable of seduction, kidnapping, and killing. One morally ambiguous scene shows Jessica stealing money with a gang of thugs in order to pay for Niki's son's school tuition.

Much of the viewing audience seems to relate to the moral ambiguity of the show. One *Heroes* blogger wrote, "One of the things I really love about the characters in *Heroes* is that things are rarely, if ever, black and white."[13] What this blogger and most other viewers like about the moral ambiguity of *Heroes*, no doubt, is that it reflects reality. Sure, the characters can do unreal things like zap their enemies and stop time, but their moral grayness is certainly real. In fact, one of the most common assumptions in a moral debate today is that, while some moral decisions are black and white, most of what goes on is a big fat cloud of gray.

In other words, there is no clear-cut answer to some questions of moral importance.

The obvious rejoinder is that moral decisions appear gray, not because they aren't black or white, but because they're both black *and* white. When you print a shade of gray in a book or a newspaper, the printer doesn't lather a nice dollop of gray ink on the paper; it fakes it by printing finely spaced dots of black on white paper. The result is a perception of gray that's really made up of black and white.

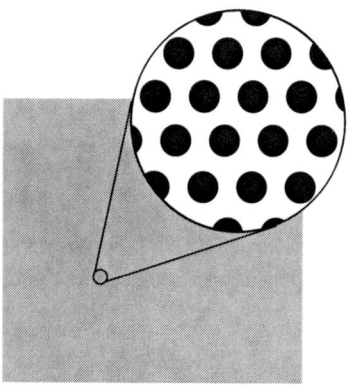

Fig. 10. In printing, a field of gray is really composed of aspects of black and white.

Similarly, moral decisions that appear unclear are not really morally ambiguous; they're just extremely complex combinations of morally clear positions. For instance, the decision to give money to a homeless person could be morally confusing and involve many separate moral decisions. The individual implications involved in giving money to a homeless person (let's call him Bob) could be to: help Bob eat (good), reduce the desire for Bob to help himself (bad), give to the poor (good), prevent that money from going to a potentially worthier cause (bad), support a corrupt welfare system (bad), help get Bob back on his feet (good), possibly contribute to an alcohol or drug addiction (bad), and save Bob's life (good). Clearly, giving someone on the street a few dollars for food is not as simple as it seems—in some ways the decision can be seen as morally gray. There are pluses and minuses in this theoretical dilemma, and to make a decision one must calculate the balance of good and bad in the act or ignore most of the constituent decisions that go with the act of giving money to Bob.

In an effort to save some time, I won't do the cost-benefit analysis of the act of giving money to homeless Bob. But the problem with such an analysis remains: it's tough to do, especially if it's required for all of life's decisions. We don't have time to break out an Excel spreadsheet every time we encounter a moral dilemma in our lives.

Luckily, we don't have to; our brains do much of the heavy calculating without much effort on our parts as the result of a little skill we call intuition. Our intuition, or gut reaction, to most moral questions is usually right. We know this because many studies have shown that there's a lot more going on in our brains than we are conscious of.

Edward Katkin and colleagues at the University of New York at Stony Brook showed subjects a series of images that were too brief to recognize consciously and accompanied some of the images with electric shocks.[14] The researchers found that the subjects were able to predict when they'd receive a shock based on their subconscious reactions to certain images. They didn't consciously register the visual cues, but they knew what was going on subconsciously. In other words, our subconscious minds lead to gut reactions for things we're not completely aware of, but which we can consider good or bad.

In addition, many studies have shown that our subconscious minds work well even when our conscious minds don't. Another study conducted at the University of Florida looked at people who have suffered damage to a specific area of the brain involved in face recognition (a condition called prosopagnosia) and are unable to consciously identify whether or not they've seen a particular face before. Something in the patient's brain is active, however, because when they see someone they've met before, their body displays signs of recognition (increased perspiration and pulse) despite the fact that they don't consciously recognize the person.[15] These patients may not consciously know that they know this person, but, thanks to their subconscious minds, they react like they do. Intuition is not completely understood by the scientific community, but it's becoming accepted that intuition is the brain's way of summarizing the knowledge of a lifetime into one quick instruction. As Gary Klein says about gut feelings in his book *The Power of Intuition*, "You better take them seriously because they reflect all of your experiences."[16]

That's just the point. We can't possibly mull over all of our knowledge each time we make a decision, so we must rely on our subconscious minds to group the information and give us a good estimate of what we should do. This estimate usually tends to be accurate. When we make the mistake of thinking that we can't make good decisions based on everything we've learned because we can't possibly retrieve all that information, we're forgetting that we have a very powerful and efficient subconscious, as well as conscious, mind.

If the gray swatch above represents a moral decision, each constituent decision involved is reflected in either a black dot or a white space. Our conscious mind looks at the black and white areas and confuses them as gray; but, with regards to morality, our subconscious mind computes the moral implications and rounds them to a final decision. The TV show *Heroes* attempts to show that there may be good and bad in any given situation, but, as we will see, if something is wrong, it is always wrong regardless of the good it produces. Jessica's stealing is still wrong even though it pays for her alter ego's son's education. If your gut doesn't tell you that, perhaps a bald guy with a toga might convince you.

everything i learned, i taught myself

On a Friday afternoon in a third-grade class in a typical American suburb, Rick Garlikov experienced an amazing act of education. The class of twenty-two children learned binary arithmetic, a form of math using just the two digits zero and one (zero is 0, one is 1, two is 10, three is 11, four is 100, etc.). The children went from knowing nothing of the subject to being able to multiply complex binary numbers within the course of half an hour. Binary math is a difficult concept for many adults to grasp, and, before the lesson, the third-grade teacher predicted that only two students would be able to understand the material. But all the kids were interested, soaking up the material like little sponges with Pokémon backpacks. The interesting thing isn't that the kids

122 - science, socrates, and sense

learned the material, though, or even that they were totally engrossed in it; rather, it was that the third graders taught binary arithmetic to themselves.

How did a bunch of little rugrats teach themselves how to add and multiply in the language of computers and other electronics, you ask? Writer Rick Garlikov simply posed the children a series of questions that led them to draw conclusions on this complex subject by themselves. In essence, Garlikov used the process known as the Socratic method to let the youngsters develop the ideas on their own. Throughout the class, Garlikov didn't tell the kids a thing; he just asked questions (seventy-six questions, to be exact).

> *Rick Garlikov (RG): How come we have ten numerals? Could it be because we have ten fingers?*
> *Children (C): Could be.*
> *RG: What if we were aliens with only two fingers? How many numerals might we have?*
> *C: Two.*
> *RG: How many numbers could we write out of two numerals?*
> *C: Not many.*
> *One kid: There would be a problem.*
> *RG: What problem?*
> *One kid: They couldn't do this. [He holds up seven fingers]*
> *RG: Okay, what can we write as we count? [Writes as they call out answers.]*
> *C: Zero, one . . . [Silence]*
> *RG: Is that it? What do we do on this planet when we run out of numerals at nine?*
> *C: Write down "one, zero."*
> *RG: Why?*
> *C: [almost in unison] I don't know; that's just the way you write "ten."*[17]

Rick and the children continued in this manner until the third graders had grasped the concept that we can use different written systems to represent the same numbers. Near the end of the half hour, the class had figured out what the number ten looks like in binary form (it's 1010), and the children were enthralled. Garlikov asked them how many numbers they thought they could write with a one and a zero. "Mega-zillions" was their answer.

> *RG: There, now you know how to do it. Of course, until you get used to reading numbers this way, you need your chart, because it is hard to read something like "10011001011" in alien, right?*
> *C: Right.*
> *RG: So who uses this stuff?*
> *C: Nobody/aliens.*
> *RG: No, I think you guys use this stuff every day. When do you use it?*
> *C: No, we don't.*
> *RG: Yes, you do. Any ideas where?*
> *C: No.*
> *RG: [Walks over to the light switch and, pointing to it, asks:] What is this?*
> *C: A switch.*
> *RG: [Flips it off and on a few times.] How many positions does it have?*
> *C: Two.*
> *RG: What could you call these positions?*
> *C: On and off/up and down.*
> *RG: If you were going to give them numbers what would you call them?*
> *C: One and two.*
> *One student: OH!! ZERO AND ONE!*
> *All the kids then: OH, YEAH!* [17]

Granted, Garkilov assisted the children in their lesson. It's not likely that the children would have come up with binary math on their own even if they wanted to for some strange reason, but the children did come to all the conclusions themselves—no one had to teach them the material in the traditional sense of the word. They learned the material, and they were enthusiastic about it. At the end of the class, Garlikov reported that "at least nineteen of the twenty-two students had fully and excitedly participated and absorbed the entire material." Remember that, initially, the teachers predicted that only two students would grasp the material.

This example shows us two important things about concurrence. First, binary math demonstrates nicely the concept of a monospective. Our culturally derived labels don't fully represent the concepts they are meant to. For example, we can write the concept of two with the digit "2," but we can also write it in binary with "10." "2" and "10" are two different labels for the same concept. Just as the religious practitioners used different words to label the same spiritual phenomenon, we can use different labels to represent the same mathematical concept, too.

Second, the Socratic method reveals an important aspect of human cognition: we can only fully understand something if we arrive at it ourselves, not just when someone tells us it is so. As a friend of mine who is a marriage and family therapist said, "It is much more beneficial for a client to come to an understanding on their own, rather than being told what to do or how to think about something." And Garlikov added that the Socratic method serves "as a logical, incremental, step-wise guide that enables students to figure out about a complex topic or issue with their own thinking and insights."[17]

It's important to know if we really understand something or

if we're just repeating what we hear the teacher say. There is a clear difference; for instance, we can say that the number ten in binary is "1010" by repeating what a teacher tells us, but to understand that ten can be expressed as "1010" because 1010 equals one eight (the first digit in "1010"), no fours (second digit), one two (third digit), and zero ones (fourth digit) in the number ten. The difference between memorization and understanding in a topic like this is like the difference between Salieri's euphoric reaction to sheet music compared with my blank stare.

	8s	4s	2s	1s	binary equivalent
one				1	1
two			1	0	10
four		1	0	0	100
five		1	0	1	101
nine	1	0	0	1	1001
ten	1	0	1	0	1010

Fig. 11. Binary shows how we can use two different labels to identify the same concept (e.g., 10 and 1010 for the concept of ten.

The Socratic method allows us to come to the same conclusion about the subject as the person who understands it already—in a sense, it's a method for merging two distinct perspectives into one *panspective*. This is why the Socratic method is such a common way of teaching in law school and why seemingly all of the television commercials aired today end with a question like "Got milk?" or "Wanna get away?" Both the law instructor and the advertiser want you to feel or understand that which they already know, and so they pose a question and let you come to the desired conclusion yourself; they engage your creative problem-solving mind—your ah-ha brain region—and not just your memorization skills. The Socratic method is also the best way to achieve concurrence on a particular discussion or argument. If you want convey the morality of not stealing, pose the question, "How would you feel if someone stole *your* Huffy ten-speed?" Or, in order to agree about whether Mr. X is a good candidate, ask your companion what makes a good government servant. And if you find that you disagree with someone about God, ask him, "What is God?"

The Socratic method also points to an interesting question in itself. Is there an objective truth to things? Garlikov didn't tell the third graders how to multiply binary digits; he *asked* them. In fact, no one told them—yet they came to the conclusion themselves. They found the solution to the problem presented just as Schelling's students came to the same conclusion about where to meet in New York City. The third graders' focal points were their common answers, just as Grand Central Station was the focal point for Schelling's students. If a third-grade class can come to the same intelligent conclusions about binary mathematics as computer scientists on their own and not through instruction, an objective truth seems likely. We've seen that people can agree on where to meet a stranger in New York and what type of numerals an alien would use, but is there a focal point for all of human morality? As I will show in the next section, the answer is yes, and the proof may be found in disagreement, of all places.

he said, she said

I can't say that the thirty-two-inch screen in my living room displays much reality television these days, but when it does I can't help but notice that the bulk of shows like *The Real World*, *The Osbournes*, or *Survivor* consists of bickering between the characters. Questions like "Why are you talking trash behind my back?" or "Why'd you let Minnie chew on the furniture?" and "Can't you gather more than one coconut a day?!" abound on the mindless but addictive shows. Most people agree that reality television is about as *real* as Michael Jackson's nose, but they might also add that the bickering aspect is a fairly accurate portrayal of real life—after all, that's what drunk twenty-somethings, British rock star families, and people stranded on a desert island do; they bicker.

Nearly everyone bickers on a regular basis. Arguing over petty things—bickering—occurs in the office, between spouses, and even between strangers in everyday situations. Reality television is entertaining partly because it showcases some bizarre human beings doing some crazy things, but also because it reflects the very common and relatable act of bickering.

But, despite the ubiquity of nagging, nitpicking, and quarrelling in today's society, none of these seem to do much good. People get mad while bickering; they ruin perfectly good relationships over little squabbles; and they sometimes resort to violence over a petty disagreement. Little fights never seem to be resolved and just tend to foster animosity between people. But there are benefits to getting worked up about the little stuff. An argument helps its participants to define and refine their positions; it helps people to achieve a sense of their individuality; and it allows the arguers the ability to express feelings that they wouldn't express under normal circumstances. As developmental psychologist Annie Rogers of Hampshire College in Amherst put it, "When you fight, you push yourself and the other person to a rawness of feeling, where you say more than you otherwise would."[18]

Bickering also points to an interesting aspect of the truth—it shows that both people involved believe that it exists. Because both parties in an argument are emphatically trying to show that the other person is in the wrong, there must be a right in their minds. Why would a participant on *The Real World* complain about being talked about behind her back if she didn't think that doing so was wrong? Why would Jack Osbourne protest the family dog's extracurricular chewing if it were not causing some sort of injustice? And why would the *Survivor* contestant object when another contestant collects just one coconut if there wasn't a higher standard—at least in his mind—to be met? Sure, reality TV characters may bicker just to hear themselves talk and to give the audience a show, but, in real life, people complain, protest, and object to others' behavior because they are sure that there is an objective standard. And they are equally sure that standard is not being met. As C. S. Lewis put it, "Quarrelling means trying to show that the other man is in the wrong. And there would be no sense in trying to do that unless you and he had some sort of agreement as to what Right and Wrong are."[18] Indeed, there wouldn't. The complaint is a real-world whistle blown to call a foul. If there weren't a rule with regard to the situation, there would be no reason to blow the whistle.

The instigator is usually right to believe there is an objective standard that those involved should follow, and the accused usually provides proof of that standard. When one person accuses another of failing to meet a behavioral standard, the defendant usually tries to show his adherence to the standard he's accused of breaking; rarely does he ever say, "I don't give a lick about your standard." Meanwhile, in defending himself according to the standard, he's accepting that the standard—a moral truth—actually exists.

Sometimes people will admit to breaking a certain standard but justify their behavior with an example of another broken standard. "I didn't tip the waiter because I just got laid off," "I hit my son because he painted the dog with ketchup," or "I threw Brutus to the ground because he stepped on my toe" are examples of retaliatory action. But, again, the defendant usually admits that a wrong was committed; it just so happens that there was a good reason for it—it was in reaction to another injustice. As we will see later, the old adage "two wrongs don't make a right" holds true, but the acknowledgment of both wrongs in this situation shows that there is an objective standard that is not being followed.

Bickering and quarrelling aren't the only instances in which an objective moral standard shows up. Most people believe in fairness as an objective truth, and they work to promote it even at the risk of financial sacrifice. In an experiment called the ultimatum game, researchers invited two people to share $10. One of the participants (randomly selected) got to choose how the two should split the reward, and the other participant could accept or reject the offer. If the offer were accepted, the two would go home with the designated amount; if the second participant rejected the offer, they both would leave the experiment with nothing. Theoretically, the first person should be able to split the reward $9 to $1, and the second person should accept because a lone dollar is better than nothing. But when participants were offered an unfair amount (i.e., the participant making the offer proposed to keep more than $6), the offer was routinely rejected. The second participant in the experiment found disproportionate offers to be unfair and forced the other to go home empty-handed to pay for his greed, despite the fact that it meant he would go home empty-handed, too. This shows that people are willing to put their money where their mouths are with regard to fairness.[19]

A critic might say that people abide by moral standards when the potential reward can buy a gallon of gas, but what if the reward could buy an entire car? Would people be so moral if the stakes were raised? That's what other researchers sought to find out in Indonesia, where citizens, on average, received an income of less than $700 during the year of 1994. Researchers conducted the ultimatum game with participants, sometimes offering the equivalent of a few months' wages to the pair of participants. It turns out that participants still rejected offers below 20 percent of the entire reward.[20] Participants did accept lower offers more readily when the stakes were higher, but they maintained a high standard of fairness even when they could have pocketed a substantial, but unfair, amount of cash. The most interesting thing about this study, however, isn't how many unfair offers were rejected; it's how many unfair offers were made. Even with high stakes—when the proposer had a much better chance to act unfairly—nearly half offered a fifty-fifty split. For the most part, the proposer chose fairness over greed. It appears, at least in some cases, that our moral compass remains focused even when the direction of greed is extremely tempting.

There is a moral standard outside of economics games, too. In a comprehensive survey of studies, political science professor Donald Kinder found that people vote for candidates and electoral propositions they think are morally right, not just those which will personally benefit them. On affirmative action, Kinder found that "white and black Americans come to their views without calculating personal harms or benefits."[21] Parents with school children don't necessarily support more government aid to education. And draft-age citizens don't oppose military conflicts more than other Americans. In fact, Kinder found that personal interest was of little importance on most political issues, from racial busing to gun control. One would think that voters would vote to benefit themselves and would disregard an objective moral standard, but that is not the case. People vote for what's right, not necessarily what benefits them personally. Just like the bickerers and the ultimatum game participants, voters do know that there is indeed a right and a wrong. Now if we could only agree on what that right and wrong is.

onward

We live in a society that is inundated with the scourge of moral relativism despite its innate contradictions. Hopefully, in this part, I've been able to show that, while moral relativism has its appeal in a divisive, antagonistic society, it is not the answer. Using the scientific model of an ultimate truth, we can seek a universal truth in morality also. From science, we can see that judgment, while it has its limitations, is useful in gaining truth. But in order to make a worthwhile judgment, the judge must be open-minded. As in science, moral judgments must rely on all available information and be turned over as soon as contrary information appears on the scene.

Some judgments are seemingly impossible to make, which is why many of us turn to moral relativism in the first place. But, as was shown, morally gray situations aren't really gray; instead, they're very complex combinations of black and white. There is a truth in every situation and in every moral choice. The fact that we can come to the same conclusions independent of strict instructions (through the Socratic method) shows us that once we merge perspectives, this truth, or panspective, becomes clearer. Further proof of an objective truth comes, surprisingly, from the fact that we argue. If there wasn't some standard to which to compare our actions, what use would there be in trying to convince someone that the standard hadn't been met?

Hopefully, I've shown that there is an objective truth out there that should be used to measure our behavior. In the next part, I will show how this objective truth—this panspective—doesn't just condemn commonly agreed-upon evils like lying and enslavement, but it expressly describes *why* they are wrong. As we'll see, the universal morality can show you how to tackle almost any moral dilemma and can reveal that someone you know may be morally on par with the architects of the Enron debacle. This universal morality shows that consistency is the key to goodness in our behavior. We've acknowledged the existence of the moral Mauna Kea; shall we ascend it?

part IV

misdemeanors, machiavelli, and morality

Cannonballs fell like hail on Fort Sumter federal military base in South Carolina, and the newly inaugurated President Abraham Lincoln was left with one of the greatest moral dilemmas any American has ever faced. Lincoln had to decide whether to declare war on the seceded states or suffer the breakup of the Union and allow the morally reprehensible practice of human slavery to continue to blight the continent. The secession was predicated on President Lincoln's stance that the "government cannot endure permanently half slave, half free."[1] Lincoln was going to abolish slavery, and the Southern states, which avidly defended their barbaric behavior, weren't going to let him do it.

Even before the Sumter attack, a bloody conflict seemed inevitable. The country was severely divided on the issue of slavery, and neither side appeared willing to give in. Monumental moral dualism had been established, and the entire country was engulfed in an us-against-them mentality. Lincoln was left with two options: allow secession and slavery or declare war. He opted for war.

Lincoln's dilemma is similar to so many moral dilemmas, both historic and hypothetical, that present two decisions—each with negative outcomes—as the only options for action. A hypothetical situation that reflects Lincoln's dilemma is the hungry caveman example. In it, a hungry caveman needs to feed himself and his family. Food is hard to come by in the Ice Age in which he lives, so when he notices his neighbor preparing two tasty-looking legs of mutton for dinner, he contemplates his options. He could turn away and risk starvation for his family, or he could kill his neighbor and take the tasty legs of mutton. Both scenarios are unpleasant and both result in unfortunate prehistoric character dying. Is there a morally right choice in a dilemma like this in which both options are so unappealing?

Such dilemmas are difficult to find the right answer to because they don't have a clear solution. An economist might relate these types of decisions to a zero-sum game in which, if there is a winner, there must also be a loser. For example, slicing an apple pie represents a zero-sum situation; the larger slice one person cuts for himself, the smaller everyone else's piece must be. Of course, the choices between war and slavery or starvation and killing are a bit more dramatic than slicing apple pie or even the win-lose games like chess and tennis described in the Introduction. Worse, they're more like lose-lose games in which there isn't a real winner. Dilemmas like Lincoln's lead people to believe that we live in a morally gray world in which we must do some wrong to produce any good or even exist at all. After all, it's generally accepted that Lincoln had to either fight a war or allow slavery—both morally reprehensible options.

However, as we saw in the previous part, moral decisions aren't gray; they are just complex combinations of black and white. Every moral dilemma, including Lincoln's and the starving caveman's, has a definitive moral right and wrong, and the key to figuring out the moral solution is revealed in a paradigm shift of sorts. As we'll see, we can shift our mentality from a zero-sum framework to a non-zero-sum framework, and, when we do, a clear moral solution presents itself. That is what I hope to show in this part of *Everyone Agrees*. By the end of this part, I hope to convey the idea that there is one simple rule that helps to explain the right and wrong in every moral situation—the panspective, or Mauna Kea, of the theory of concurrence.

To explain this panspective, I will look at the three principles of concurrence as applied to morality and show how they apply to everyday (and not-so-everyday) moral decisions. Standing on the shoulders of one particularly short man with very large ideas (Immanuel Kant), we will see the intricacies of a universal morality—a belief system on which we can all agree. There is a logical system that can help us to make moral decisions and give us insight into some of the most gut-wrenching of dilemmas, like Lincoln's. But before I describe concurrence as it applies to morality, I'd like to explain what it is not, namely utilitarianism and the Golden Rule. Utilitarianism (the idea that the moral value of an action is determined by its contribution to the overall happiness of the population) cannot be utilized for our purposes, and the well-known Golden Rule doesn't quite measure up.

slap happy

On April 30, 2004, one of the most damaging computer viruses ever, SASSER, was released over the Internet. SASSER completely disrupts a user's computer and sends copies of itself to random computers linked to the Internet.[2] Shortly after the release of the virus, the French News Agency was infected and its satellites were blocked, many transatlantic flights were cancelled, banks were closed, and some hospitals had to redirect patients because their systems had been disabled. Estimates of tens of millions of PCs were affected, and countless man-hours were lost in fixing the damage.[3]

Eventually, friends of the culprit tipped off authorities, and the police found and arrested the troublemaker. He was a seventeen-year-old "computer enthusiast" from Germany, evidently with a little too much time on his hands. After the arrest, the hacker's stepmother recalled how he had talked to his dad about his devious little plan. "Papa," he said, "I've put out a computer worm."[4] His dad asked him if he had done anything stupid, and the stepmother recalled that the young man had just kind of laughed nervously in response.

Almost four years later, on the other side of the Atlantic, a seven-year-old child decided that he had had enough of the drama in his house, so he took the keys to his grandmother's Dodge Durango and drove off with a friend. Not even half the legal driving age, the kid peered over the steering wheel and actually drove a few miles, knocking over several mailboxes and running into a number of parked cars in the nearby Costco parking lot. The little joyride ended when the seven-year-old ran into a curb and snapped off one of the car's axles. Luckily, no one was hurt in the incident.[5]

When police questioned the boy as to why he took part in such a reckless, potentially catastrophic act, he replied, "I wanted to do it because it's fun. Fun to do bad things."[6] Indeed. Surely it was fun right until the child's grandmother got home and "whipp[ed] his behind."[6] When a policeman asked the child if he thought he should be punished for his behavior, the child responded, "Just a little bit—no video games for a whole weekend."[6]

Besides having too much free time, the kids in these stories have something in common—something very troubling. The computer hacker didn't gain financially from his virus; he didn't help put food on his table; and he didn't garner a good reputation for his family. He caused all that trouble because it made him happy in a twisted sort of way ("Look, papa! I stopped the world for a few hours!"). The American kid who took his grandma's car for a joyride did so for a similar reason: not because it helped anyone in any way, but because it was fun. The kids' behavior shows that happiness, while generally a good thing, cannot be the sole criteria for a universal morality.

Philosopher Blaise Pascal once said, "All men seek happiness. This is without exception. Whatever different means they employ, they all tend to this end. The cause of some going to war, and of others avoiding it, is the same desire in both, attended with different views."[7] And this can hardly be refuted. People are constantly trying to make themselves happy, whether by sensual pleasures, social status, or the noble pride of having helped someone else in need. Simply put, happiness is the most basic and ubiquitous goal for mankind. It is this reasoning that led people like Jeremy Bentham to promote the philosophy of utilitarianism, which posits that the moral value of an act depends on its contribution to the sum of all happiness. Many people today, whether moral dualists or moral relativists, agree—if it feels good, why not?

But can we rely on utilitarianism as a sound moral philosophy for everyone? We can all agree that happiness is everyone's goal, but the things that make people happy are as varied as the population itself, and those happiness generators can sometimes create bewilderment. As Pascal noted, happiness is even the motive of the person who hangs himself.

Babies are happy when someone makes a silly face or a funny noise at them; tennis players are happy when they finally win a Grand Slam tournament; and benevolent people are happy when they help others find a meal. But a thief is happy when his loot is more valuable than expected; a masochist is happy when he hurts himself; and some kids are happy when they spread a harmful computer virus or run their grandma's car into the ground. This wide-open, arbitrary nature of happiness precludes it from being the ultimate goal of morality. When a feeling like happiness rewards positive behavior, like feeding the hungry, as well as dreadful actions, like destroying someone else's car, it cannot be the objective good that we are seeking as the universal morality.

Of course, Jeremy Bentham made sure to note that it is the *sum* of all happiness that is the goal of humanity. Since the child criminals above caused more unhappiness in the world than happiness, their actions can be considered wrong to the utilitarian. But what if the computer virus infected only one person's computer, or the seven-year-old damaged only his grandma's car and not the others? Both are cases of one person's happiness versus another's. In the car situation, it could be argued that more happiness was gained in the transaction than lost if the kid had a really good time on his joyride and his grandma didn't mind getting her car's axle placed back on the car. What if someone would enjoy the clothes you're wearing more than you? Does that give him the right to take the shirt off your back? According to utilitarianism, if more happiness is gained by the transaction, it is morally beneficial. As you can see, this won't do—we can't have people stripping others of their clothes just because it makes them happy, and we can't have children taking destructive joyrides or sending out harmful computer viruses just because doing so puts a wicked grin on their faces. Sadly, happiness does not lead to a universal morality; there is another ethic that explains right and wrong more effectively. Perhaps the metaphorical peak of Mauna Kea is gilded? We shall see.

the golden age

So what *is* the objective moral standard that governs everyone silently if not our agreed goal of happiness? While no one has really pinpointed what an agreed objective morality might look like, many have given it a name. Ancient Asians called it the Tao, or the way—that which was present before the creator. Aristotle called it the law of nature, a law that should be applied universally. And Christian thinker C. S. Lewis called it the moral law, an innate feeling that tells us to do the right thing when faced with a moral dilemma. When people do try to quantify a universal morality, they usually boil it down to one universal commandment: do unto others as you would have done unto you. This is the Golden Rule.

The above rule is, of course, the Christian version of the expression; there are many other manifestations. From 1000 BC, the Jewish Bible states, "Thou shalt love thy neighbor as thyself."[8]

In 500 BC, Confucius commanded, "What you do not want others to do to you, do not do to others."[8] One hundred and fifty years later, the moral reverberated through Greece when Isocrates said, "Do not do to others what would anger you if done to you by others."[8] The ancient Indian text *The Mahabharata* offered virtually the same expression as did the Christian Bible in various places. Muslim an-Nawawi quotes the prophet, saying, "None of you [truly] believes until he wishes for his brother what he wishes for himself."[8] And the same sentiment is repeated in every moral code from ancient Egyptian to modern Humanism. In fact, most people, when asked to come up with a lone rule to govern everyone effectively, would come up with the same thing: the Golden Rule.

While everyone can generally agree that the Golden Rule is the best single law to dictate behavior, it's unclear what behavior it actually promotes. If you find a wallet on the street containing the owner's phone number and $100 in cash, the Golden Rule easily applies: call the owner and return the cash because that's what you would want to be done for you. But when moral dilemmas get trickier, the Golden Rule isn't as decisive. Imagine an overcrowded lifeboat that will sink if people aren't thrown overboard into icy waters. The dilemma is: throw some poor passengers off or let everyone sink. If you apply the Golden Rule to this dilemma, you won't throw anyone overboard because you wouldn't want that for yourself; but you would be obligated to throw someone over because everyone would sink otherwise, a result that no one wants.

The above scenario actually happened in 1841 when the American ship *William Brown* hit an iceberg and sank quickly.[9]

The crew and passengers were crammed into two lifeboats, the larger of which was manned by seaman Alexander Holmes. At one point, freezing rain began to pour down on the survivors, the waves picked up, and the boat began to fill with water. Holmes and his crew threw sixteen people into the brutally cold water, sealing their fate, but perhaps saving the rest of the survivors. Those who remained on the boat were eventually rescued, but Holmes was put on trial and found guilty of manslaughter when he returned to England. The question remains: was Holmes's decision to jettison some of the passengers the right thing to do? Unfortunately, the Golden Rule is powerless in situations like this.

The problem with the Golden Rule is that it relies on a subjective moral standard, not an objective one. The Golden Rule cannot solve moral dilemmas like the lifeboat example above, and in fact, the rule leads to objectively negative consequences when applied to other situations. Despite the widely held belief that people always want to benefit themselves, there are some who would actually harm themselves, for whatever reason; and by applying the Golden Rule, they could be justified in harming another person. For instance, according to the Golden Rule, it would be acceptable for someone to smoke a cigarette in a crowded elevator (harming others) if he or she would accept others doing the same thing. A towering football player may enjoy roughhousing with other likewise large human beings, but when that desire sprouts in the company of normal-sized people, the results could be damaging to everyone who doesn't enjoy the company of large colliding beasts. And someone with very little money could justify stealing from a wealthy woman by claiming that, if he was that rich, he would *give* his money to the poor. People vary in terms of their personal preferences and their tolerances for different situations. Since the Golden Rule is based on that unstable standard of personal preference, it fails to be objective.

A relative of mine used to play in the premier division of college basketball, a game in which it is officially illegal to intentionally hit an opponent with an elbow or any other appendage. My relative, however, admitted that he would take cheap shots at defenders as he was going up for a basket because, as he explained it, he was going to receive the same treatment from the other team—it was expected. According to the Golden Rule, my relative wasn't doing anything wrong when he intentionally elbowed his opponent if he expected the same treatment in return. I, on the other hand, wouldn't elbow my opponent on my way to a two-point dunk shot, and I would expect not to be elbowed at the other end of the court. However, if I were to play my relative in basketball, we would have conflicting standards of right and wrong, and I might end up with a bruised jaw even if we both agreed on the Golden Rule.

The difficulty with the Golden Rule is that, while everyone may agree on it as a universal standard for morality, it leaves the approved behavior up in the air. The Golden Rule relies on the whims of the people involved; thus, it is not objective. Moreover, the reason there is so much quarreling and bickering throughout society could in fact stem from the Golden Rule itself. With the Golden Rule, everyone argues about whether something is right or wrong according to *them*; they don't look to an objective standard. This is forgivable, since no objective standard exists—or does it? In the next section, I hope to uncover an objective moral standard that applies to every situation and every personal temperament.

the theory of concurrence applied to morality

In 1936, the central authority of the Soviet Union sought out the opinion of the citizenry for the formulation of a new constitution. Throughout the summer and fall of that year, local administrators across the country pulled nearly 80 percent of the population into forums to discuss and offer suggestions about the unprecedented constitution. While many of the citizens' suggestions were largely ignored in the final draft, the 1936 constitution ended up enumerating a clear list of individual civil rights, theretofore absent from Soviet governance.

In the new document, referred to by many as the Stalin constitution, the right to "universal, equal and direct suffrage by secret ballot" was guaranteed, as was freedom to assemble, freedom of the press, freedom to protest, and freedom of religion.[10] In addition, these rights were guaranteed for every citizen regardless of sex, race, or ethnicity. From the looks of things, the new constitution was a giant step toward freedom for the socialist state.

However, once the 1936 constitution was approved, the Soviet government pretty much disregarded the entire thing. People could vote, but there was only one candidate for each election. Government officials heavily censored the press and arrested protesters. Religious persecution was rampant, as was ethnic cleansing.[11] The Soviet government was completely contradicting itself, and, in many cases, the contradiction was clearly documented. For example, in one constitutional article, citizens were obliged to safeguard and strengthen socialist property; meanwhile, another article claimed there would be no socialist ownership and recognized the rights of personal ownership for individuals.

What is a citizenry to think when confronted with such paradoxical laws and governance? How can people enforce such a contradictory atmosphere, much less live under it and thrive? The answer, of course, is that they can't—at least not for very long. The Soviet system was great at getting every ounce of effort out of a coerced people; but after decades of contradictory governance, the Soviet state could not continue, and it imploded. The Soviet failure is proof that a contradictory government cannot exist for long.

On the other hand, a system of governance that is concurrent—one that is consistent with itself—can exist and thrive ad infinitum. For example, the U.S. Constitution operates on the basic principle that people are free to do what they want as long as their behavior doesn't interfere with the freedoms of others—a truly consistent framework.

And that framework has proved to be long lasting. While the United States is in its relative infancy compared to some Asian and European nations, and while its government is surely becoming more contradictory with each approved government bailout and infringement of natural rights, the basic governing system on which it operates has outlasted most others since 1789. The Soviet Union lasted a mere seventy-four years compared to the two-centuries-plus of American stability. China and India look completely different from what they were in the eighteenth century, too. And the quintessential European state, France, has endured numerous revolutions and monarchies, five different republican governments with different hierarchies of power, as well as a variety of totalitarian and socialist systems since the United

States began its present form of government centuries ago.[12]

A law or collection of laws can be seen as good or bad based on one's perspective. For instance, a law that prohibits skateboarders from doing their thing on playground equipment is good for the family using the playground equipment as it was intended to be used, but that same law is bad for the kid on the skateboard who wants to pull an airwalk grab off of the same equipment. Similarly, an international law, like the United Nations Security Council Resolution 1441, which forced Iraq to submit to the inspection of various Iraqi facilities by UN regulators as a "final opportunity to comply,"[13] was good for the international community but bad for Iraq, which no doubt saw the law as an affront to its sovereignty. Both of these laws are subjectively good or bad, depending on the perspective with which one is viewing them. But is there such a thing as an *objectively* good or bad law? If so, by what standard can this be determined?

There is such a thing as an objectively good or bad law, and there is only one standard by which a law can be measured. Since external parties can view laws differently, the standard of objectivity must be found not externally, but internally. If a law or collection of laws is consistent with itself, it can be considered objectively good; conversely, if a law is contradictory, it can be considered objectively bad.

This concept applies to much more than skateboarding laws and UN resolutions., though. The consistency/contradiction dichotomy that we see in government also applies to morality as a whole; in fact, it comprises the first principle of the theory of concurrence as applied to morality:

I. an act that is concurrent is innately right, and an act that is contradictory is innately wrong.

In other words, an act must agree with itself, at the very least, to be considered morally right. If someone has a moral dilemma, the choice that provides no contradiction is the only moral act. This principle is based heavily on the tall idea of a short Prussian man who lived in the nineteenth century, Immanuel Kant. Kant wrote a treatise on morality, *Groundwork of the Metaphysics of Morals*, which was as revolutionary to the field of philosophy as it was difficult to read. Despite the unimpressive prose, Kant is regarded as one of the most influential thinkers of his time, mainly because he devised a proof for morality unlike anything seen before. The proof was the universality test, in which Kant encourages us to "act so that [your action] may be capable of becoming a universal law for all rational beings."[14] If one can apply an action universally without contradiction, he wrote, it is moral.[15]

To demonstrate this, I'd like to evoke a relic from the corporate scandals of the early twenty-first century, the Enron debacle. Kenneth Lay was the CEO of Enron Corporation leading up to the accounting scandal that shook corporate American and devastated the lives of thousands of employees and investors through lies and fraud. Lay sought to deceive stockholders about Enron's balance sheets in order to artificially inflate the stock price so that he could cash out on stock options with heavily overvalued shares (evidently the $42.4 million compensation package he received in 1999[16] wasn't enough to suffice his greed).

Let's assume that Lay was earnestly confused about the morality of lying about the balance sheets and wanted to assess whether his actions were morally right or wrong. He could use Kant's universality test by applying his behavior universally and assuming that all corporations drew up incorrect balance sheets. If that were the case, however, the entire concept of reporting those numbers would be meaningless. Consequently, no one would believe any corporate balance sheets, including Enron's, and Lay wouldn't be able to profit artificially from inflating his own accounting numbers. His deceit, if applied universally, would instantly contradict his original intent; thus, it is morally wrong.

On the other hand, corporate executives who aren't named Kenneth Lay and who choose to provide accurate balance sheets are morally right. If applied universally, providing accurate balance sheets enables trust in those balance sheets and thus reinforces the act of giving information that you want to be believed. To elaborate on this point, morally good acts naturally promote more of the same, while morally bad acts hinder the same act from happening down the line. Call it the evolution theory of morality: good acts self-perpetuate and bad acts self-destruct.

While self-perpetuation is good, if an act hurts itself in the long run, it's ultimately bad. For example, if a government passes laws that help the government to grow, they are good with respect to concurrence; but if those laws are passed at the expense of the citizenry, which the government requires to exist, then they can be considered inherently bad. For instance, a tax that wipes out the tax base is ultimately contradictory (this is reflected in the Laffer curve, the economist tool that reveals how, at some point, higher taxes decrease the incentive to work and, ultimately, decrease tax revenue).[17] Metaphorically speaking, a bear that eats a salmon is prolonging its life, but the bear that eats the *last* salmon is condemning itself to a life of starvation. A lie may be beneficial in the short term, but it may also destroy all credibility for future promises. Thus, not only do we need to be concurrent with ourselves, we also need to be concurrent with the external forces that allow us to exist.

Morality in this respect can be reduced to a simple economics coordination game. In the example described in the Introduction, the driving game, two people drive toward each other on a narrow road. When they meet, they must swerve in one direction. If the two drivers swerve in the same way, they will pass each other and go on their way; but if they swerve in opposite directions, they will crash. If the generally accepted custom were to pass to the right of oncoming traffic, the moral act (if it can be considered that) would be to go with that custom—it's the Schelling point for this decision. If, for some reason, one driver decides to go against custom and swerve to the left, the two drivers will be sorting over insurance documents instead of driving on to their destinations. If the two drivers swerve in the same direction and are consistent, the result is good; if the two drivers swerve in opposite directions and contradict each other, the result is bad. In the Enron debacle, Ken Lay contradicted the accepted custom of telling the truth and ended up metaphorically crashing head-on into oncoming moral traffic.

The skeptic would claim that Lay's immorality was only possible because of the morality of others—implying that trust begets deception. If the Enron stockholders hadn't been so trusting and honest, Lay wouldn't have been able to commit his crime. This is true, but it brings up an interesting point about concurrence: while good begets good, and evil begets evil, only good can exist without evil; the converse does not hold true. A standard of morality is required for an immoral act to transpire, but immorality is not necessary for a moral act to occur. This is represented in the second principle of the theory of concurrence applied to morality:

II. a moral act can exist independently; an immoral act requires morality to exist.

As C. S. Lewis once wrote, "Goodness is, so to speak, itself; badness is only spoiled goodness, and there must be something good first before it can be spoiled."[18] He continued by explaining that good exists on its own and evil is the parasite feeding off of that good.

One might counter that good and bad are mutually dependent; that is, if there is good, there must be bad out there somewhere. Light is only light in contrast to darkness or as the lyrics of a recent-released song argue, "you don't know how it feels to be alive until you know how it feels to die."[19] But that mentality is flawed. Light is substantial in itself, whereas darkness is only the absence of light. Similarly, life exists on its own, but something needs to be alive in order to die. Goodness is a thing in and of itself, whereas badness is only lack of goodness.

Kenneth Lay's lies were wrong because they were contradictory in nature —they failed the universality test—and because they fed off of the morality of others. But the utilitarian Jeremy Bentham might have argued that some lies, when they promote another good, are beneficial to the parties involved. For example, when great-aunt Mildred asks you whether you like the cardboard-esque fruitcake she baked, isn't a white lie a good thing if it makes Mildred feel better about herself? Moreover, aren't other immoral acts okay if they improve conditions in the long run? In other words, can't the Soviet Union espouse contradictory laws if the end result is equality and justice? Can't Lincoln go to war to save the union and stop slavery?

I can just see Niccolò Machiavelli nodding his head and grinning. The Renaissance Florentine used the zero-sum mentality to recommend that his prince take any means necessary to maintain power. Machiavelli thought that "all men are bad and ever ready to display their vicious nature, whenever they may find occasion for it."[20] So, according to Machiavelli, it's okay to be vicious right back. Cesare Borgia, for instance, was a lying and murdering duke known for his lack of scruples, yet Machiavelli commended him in *The Prince*, saying, "Borgia was reputed cruel, yet his cruelty restored Romagna, united it, and brought it to order and obedience."[20] In other words, it's okay to be immoral if you can bring order to a city; to put is succinctly, the ends justify the means. To Machiavelli, some immoral behaviors are necessary evils required to produce good.

And belief in necessary evils is as alive today as it was hundreds of years ago. For example, some people think that a 30 percent income tax is necessary if we want to live in a safe and free society. Others believe that one has to pollute the environment to produce anything worth consuming. Still others think that the death penalty is necessary to teach people that certain acts are wrong. As a Machiavellian chef might say, you have to break some eggs to make an omelet.

But while I love an omelet as much as the next person, I have to say that Machiavelli was only half right about necessary evils; they are evil, but never are they necessary. A good act that requires evil is not really good at all, and every true good can be accomplished without breaking any eggs. Machiavelli's ends-justify-the-means mentality turns a welfare state into a totalitarian regime, an innovative and healthy environment into a wasteland, and it promotes acts like suicide bombings in the name of justice. When people can rationalize bad behavior with a good end, anything can be considered morally right. Thus, the third principle of the theory of concurrence applied to morality is:

III. A moral act is good in and of itself; a right end does not justify wrong means.

There are no *necessary* evils; at least, that's what our favorite nineteenth-century philosopher, Immanuel Kant, believed. Kant would have contended that Machiavelli's philosophy was misguided and pointed out the contradiction in a moral good that requires a moral evil to exist. Kant argued that we should never use other people as a means to some other end. He wrote, "Act in such a way that you treat humanity, whether in your own person or in the person of another, always at the same time as an end and never simply as a means."[21] And this idea can be applied to all actions, not just those that involve other people. An act is moral if and only if it is good in and of itself—not as a means to some other good. Thus, Machiavelli was wrong according to Kant—Cesare Borgia's lying and murdering was not justified by his ascent to power. The Soviet Union's contradictory laws were *not* okay even though they had good intentions; Alexander Holmes's decision to throw passengers off the lifeboat was not justified by the potential for saving everyone else; and, as we'll see in the next section, Lincoln was wrong in his decision to go to war.

This principle applies to seemingly insignificant moral dilemmas as well as to life and death situations. A little white lie to great-aunt Mildred—for example, "Oh, Mildred, that fruitcake was delicious!"—may make your great-aunt feel better, but it is still a lie that will inevitably provide you with more unwanted fruitcakes in the future, wasting time and straining your interest in baked goods. On the other hand, a statement like, "You're the sweetest for thinking of me, but you know I'm not a big fan of fruitcake—it just can't compare to your sweet potato pie!" conveys your appreciation for her effort and encourages beneficial baking in the future.

Some may reason that a little white lie isn't too high a price to pay for great-aunt Mildred's happiness, but that same ends-justify-the-means mentality leads to all the moral crimes we witness today. There is no doubt that Kenneth Lay thought it was just a little white lie when he told Enron shareholders that there was "absolutely no accounting issue, no trading issue, no reserve issue, no previously unknown problem issues,"[22] prompting the departure of Jeffrey Skilling just weeks before Enron stock lost nearly all of its value. Lay was just trying to allay the fears of analysts and employees and make everyone feel better, but his lie was typical of the deceitful culture that shaped one of the largest corporate scandals of all time. Kenneth Lay's lie was wrong, as evidenced by the thousands of people who suffered financially from it, but truth still suffers when the only victim is one who bakes fruitcakes. While this consistency may seem harsh, it is the only way to avoid the arbitrary act of doing evil to promote good. Again, it's the ends-justify-the-means mentality that allows people to blow themselves up in a crowded place for some ambiguous good. Never is an evil means justified by a righteous end.

lincoln's dilemma

The U.S. Civil War lasted for four years and ravaged the entire country. 620,000 human beings were killed in battle or from disease, and another 300,000 suffered injuries, many requiring amputations. In 1863, during the middle of the war, the U.S. government estimated that it was costing the North alone $2.5 million a day. When the war ended, a final estimate put the total cost at over $6 billion. This expense was for a country with just over thirty million inhabitants and a federal government with only a $60 million budget.[23] As President Lincoln said after the first battle of the war, "It's bad. It's damned bad."[24]

But those costs were surely worth it, right? After all, slavery could not be tolerated, and Lincoln had to preserve the union. It's a given tenet of history that will be passed down through our schools as national legend; the Civil War had to happen, and we should just be glad that it ended with a unified and emancipated nation.

The choice to go to war wasn't easy. After Lincoln was elected as the first Republican president on a platform that condemned slavery, he was faced with the ultimate dilemma: he could let his country dissipate into two or more nations, or he could go to war with fellow citizens. He did not take the decision lightly, but he decided that the preservation of the union was of the utmost importance. And so the war commenced.

Hindsight is always twenty-twenty, and I have no reason to doubt that Lincoln was doing the best he knew how to do, but the American Civil War was a mistake that could have been avoided while the country achieved the same goals with a much lower cost of life. Concurrence shows us that it is contradictory (and thus morally wrong) for one human to kill another, even in war and even if the goal is as noble as preservation of a country or emancipation of slaves. Perhaps the paradoxically labeled Civil War—there's nothing civil about war—was aptly named, as I will show that the war itself was a paradox and, thus, inherently wrong. Additionally, there were other, more concurrent options for Lincoln and the Northern states, options that would have prevented such a horrific event from taking place.

Slavery was one of the ugliest evils of humanity and the most substantial blemish on an otherwise picturesque early American state. Abolition of the practice was a central theme in the newly formed Republican Party platform of 1856. The platform stated, "It is both the right and the imperative duty of Congress to prohibit in the Territories those twin relics of barbarism—Polygamy, and Slavery."[25] Lincoln ran on the idea that the country could not remain half slave states and half free. And while slavery wasn't the initial cause for the war (the preservation of the union was), it became a driving force and the eventual legacy of the brutal conflict.

But if war is the ultimate display of force over other people, how is it any better than slavery? If the Northern states wanted people to be free, why force people—sometimes even kill them—to free others? This is hypocritical and contradictory. No doubt Immanuel Kant would disapprove. But many historians and laymen claim that war was the *only* solution. Lincoln and the Union forces did what they had to do in order to free the slaves. Not quite, say others. Congressman Ron Paul said in an interview that "slavery was phased out in every other country in the world [without war]."[26] He suggested that America could have done it "like the British Empire did . . . you buy the slaves and release them." Instead of going to war, Lincoln could have emancipated the slaves and then compensated their oppressors.

It turns out that Paul's idea would have been a very smart one. There were 3,953,760[27] slaves in the United States in 1860, just before the war, and the average price of a slave was $1,658.[28] It would have cost the abolitionists around $6.5 billion to pay for the entire population—an astounding amount, but just over the amount the war ended up costing the country, anyway. If you include the cost of lives lost and emotions expended with the war, the buyout plan would have been considerably less expensive.

Lincoln didn't attack the South to end slavery, though. His main goal was to preserve the union. As Lincoln himself said, "My paramount object in this struggle is to save the Union, and is not either to save or to destroy slavery."[29] And going to war was evidently the only way to do that. Again, contradictions arise in the mentality here. Was preserving the Union so valuable that it had to happen at any cost, even if that meant the destruction of the country that made up the Union in the first place? The Northerners wanted to be united with the Southerners so much that they had to kill hundreds of thousands of them to prove it? This doesn't make sense.

Fighting someone or a group of people in order to preserve some sort of unity is the ultimate contradiction. After all, what sort of unity was left when the fighting was done—a group of exhausted, bloodied Northerners imposing their will over a group of exhausted, bloodied, and resentful Southerners? Most Southerners still didn't agree with the North after the war, but they were too tired to do anything about it. And though the Union finally emancipated the slaves, the war on fellow citizens was as much of an imposed vassalage as was the slave trade.

To many, the Civil War was a victory; the slaves were freed and the Union was preserved. But while Lincoln chose the lesser of two evils, he completely ignored the possibility of a third option that wasn't evil at all (that being the purchase and emancipation of the entire population of slaves). The same can be said of the hypothetical hungry caveman situation presented earlier. The caveman is given two options: starvation or the murder of his prehistoric neighbor for some tasty mutton, both contradictory actions. With just a little ingenuity, however, it becomes clear that he's not limited to just these two options. Instead of starving or killing his neighbor, the caveman could trade one of the extra leopard skins he has hanging around his cave (they're so 10,000 BC, anyway) for a leg of mutton. Both he and Lincoln had an option other than the two seeming lose-lose or zero-sum propositions.

We are not stuck in the zero-sum world of economics games like matching pennies or rock, paper, scissors. We live in a world where we can choose non-zero-sum solutions in which everyone wins. Lincoln had better options, the hungry caveman did not have to resort to an evil act, and, as we'll see in the next part, most of today's big moral dilemmas have non-zero-sum solutions as well. It is this non-zero approach that enables us to act concurrently; that is, to act under a universal morality. There is always a morally consistent option for our ethical dilemmas, and, if we can all agree that such an option could at least exist, we'll be well on our way to a global unity that was previously unfathomable.

onward

In 1993, Chicago hosted a convention of great ambition. Christians, Muslims, Buddhists, Jews, Sikhs, and representatives from many other religions came together in what was dubbed the Parliament of the World's Religions.[30] Under the orchestration of Hans Küng and Count von der Groeben, the various religious practitioners sought to create a united global ethic with which everyone could agree. Unlike the utilitarians, they didn't come to the conclusion that happiness was the supreme goal; nor did they simply say, "Do unto others as you would have done unto you." As we saw in the first half of this chapter, those ethics have a lot to offer, but they are not complete.

While the Parliament didn't come to one overarching concept that defined moral behavior, they did agree on four irrevocable directives: (1) respect life (thou shalt not kill); (2) deal honestly and fairly (thou shalt not steal); (3) speak and act truthfully (thou shalt not lie), and (4) respect and love one another (thou shalt not commit sexual immorality).[31] All of these were common directives throughout the ancient and modern religions, and they became the concrete foundations of the Parliament's *Towards a Global Ethic: An Initial Declaration.*

The group of religious and non-religious delegates did not mention anything about acting *consistently*, per se, but their directives are manifestations of the theory of concurrence. Each one is logical and consistent within itself; each is independent and can exist on its own; and each is good in and of itself. From the Parliament's directives, it's hard to argue with the virtues of such agreement. The only thing left to do is act consistently within that framework. As we'll see with the moral dilemmas presented in the next part, that's much easier said than done. But if representatives from all of the world's major religions can come together and agree on a lengthy declaration of morality, perhaps there's hope for the rest of us, too.

part V

destruction, dna, and deliverance

It's a dark and foggy evening and you're walking next to train tracks in a crowded city. Up ahead, a group of foolish people is walking through a long, narrow train tunnel. One of them yells out, "Look at us, we're doing something very foolish! We're walking into a narrow train tunnel. Look at us go!" Just then, you see a train barreling down on the group of people already deep into the tunnel. You look down and see a lever that would redirect the train to another track. You're not sure why the lever is there so randomly, and you can't quite make out why there's a big neon sign saying, "Pull me to save that foolish group," but, alas, there it is. And the sign is right; pulling the lever would save the group, but there's another person walking on the other track who will surely die if you do so. After wondering what's wrong with all of these fools who can't stay off of train tracks, you have to make a split-second decision to either throw the lever and save the group of people, thus sacrificing one person, or to do nothing, in which case the lone bystander will survive but everyone in the group will bite the big one. What do you do? If you're like most people, you'll pull the lever and save as many people as you can.

Now picture yourself on a bridge spanning the train tracks. The train is still barreling down on the group of people in the tunnel, and you can still avert the group casualties. But this time, in order to do so, you must push a rotund man off the bridge and onto the track below, providing a human stopper for the massive train. What would you choose to do in this scenario? If you're like most people, you'll pass on the gruesome task of sending a stranger plummeting to his death, even though doing so would save the group of people just like in the first scenario.

This is a particularly morbid thought experiment that has been conducted in every psychology office from here to Timbuktu and always elicits the same curious results. The two scenarios above are composed of the same moral tradeoff—or so it seems. In both, the subject has to choose to sacrifice one person or let a group of people die. With the first scenario, pretty much everyone agrees that it's morally acceptable to pull the lever and save the group; however, the same majority feels it would be bad to throw the stranger off the bridge for the same result. Why? This dilemma is reminiscent of the starving caveman's dilemma and Mr. Holmes's decision on the sinking lifeboat (both from the previous part), and it leads to the integral question: is it ever okay to kill someone?

The principles of concurrence described in the last part give a clear answer: no. First, the act of killing another human being fails Kant's universality test. If killing were morally acceptable, then none of us would be around long enough to talk about the morality of the act because we'd all be fighting for our own existence, not sitting around debating it. Second, human life exists independently of death (people are born without requiring a death), but death explicitly requires life to happen. Death is not independent, thus, causing death is immoral on those grounds as well. Third, and most importantly with regard to this moral dilemma, killing one to save others is not morally acceptable because it is a means to an end, not an end in itself. If this seems logical, there's a good reason. In a way, concurrence can be seen as the direct derivative of logic. An act must make sense to itself—it must be logical—for us to consider it an objective good. It would be morally right to save the group of people, but killing someone else to do so—trading life for life—just doesn't make sense.

If concurrence is so logical, then, why do moral dilemmas like the train experiment trip us up? If there is a clear distinction between what's morally right and wrong, why do most people choose to sacrifice one person for a group of people with the help of a lever, but not when we have physical contact with the victim to achieve the same goal? That's what Joshua Greene wanted to find out when he posed the dilemma to subjects as they sat very still inside a large $3 million medical device.[1] The device, better known as a functional magnetic resonance imaging (fMRI) machine, would show Greene the parts of the brain that were active while the subjects were thinking about the dilemma.

Greene found that brain regions associated with emotion (most notable was the medial frontal gyrus) were relatively quiet when subjects decided to pull the lever and save the group of people, but the same regions lit up like the fourth of July when the subjects considered physically pushing the stranger to his death in order to save the group.[2] To the subjects, the lever decision was just a mathematical equation—how can I save the most people. But those same subjects had a much more emotional reaction to the bridge scenario—how could I possibly ending someone's life? Only when they imagined actually killing someone to save others did their innate sense of right and wrong kick in. People ration, "Oh, I have to *kill* someone to save those fools? I think I'll pass."

The train dilemma presents the decision-maker with a kind of trick of the brain. Though the balance of life in both scenarios is identical, the lever option detaches the subject from the fact that he or she is really considering taking someone's life. This reveals something about the moral decision here: when we realize what we're actually doing, our humanity comes alive and our conscience steps up to the plate. As Kant professed with all immoral acts, contradictory behavior is always wrong, even if it means some good can be derived from it. Only when we trick the brain can we override our conscience to accept a morally wrong act.

But what if a madman was going to kill an innocent child? Wouldn't it be morally right to kill the madman in that situation? This question is compelling, but it showcases a problem with the above dilemma. The reason we can trick the brain in experiments like the train situation is because they are not realistic—they are, after all, purely hypothetical. Fabricated psychological dilemmas bring a complex moral decision down to a simple choice between two options, and very rarely do situations like the train dilemma come about in real life. In real life, we're not stuck with only the options to pull the lever or leave it alone; we have an infinite number of possible actions to choose from. We could pull the lever and then yell at the lone guy to get off the track; we could wave and try to get the conductor to stop the train; or we could find something else to throw on the tracks in an effort to stop the train.

In the actual case of Alexander Holmes, he could have urged the passengers of the overcrowded lifeboat to work harder in scooping out the flood water in order to keep everyone on board and alive. After all, they had survived an entire night with the same amount of people in the lifeboat; the situation couldn't have gotten so much worse as to warrant sending sixteen people into the icy waters. Scooping out the water might have been more exhausting, but at least everyone would have lived. As seen in the previous part, Lincoln also had other options besides war and letting slavery persist; he could have paid off all of the slave owners and let the Southern states try to exist without the economically superior North. As for the madman scenario above, there are other options than taking a life—there always are.

The other option is what we're looking for in this part of *Everyone Agrees*. We'll see how concurrence applies to real-life moral dilemmas—some historical, some modern. Concurrence will reveal that, while war is often seen as a necessary evil, it can never be logically acceptable and it's only understandable in self-defense. Another heated topic (no pun intended) is the environment and the energy crisis, which seems to be coming to a head with more expensive oil and political conflicts both in the Middle East and here in the United States. There have been many solutions proposed as to how we can achieve cheap, clean energy, but concurrence will show that one energy solution far outshines the others with regard to consistency. I will also commit publicity suicide and address two issues concerning life and death—abortion and the death penalty—and we'll see how each is blatantly inconsistent in a civilized society that values life. Finally, we'll look at one of the most important aspects of the universal perspective applied to our species: liberty. Interminably linked with human life and a motif that has shown up in nearly every example of this book, liberty is something on which everyone agrees.

All of these topics deserve lengthy volumes of research and debate, much more than what I will offer here, but my goal is to provide practical applications for the three principles of concurrence described in the last part, not to elaborate on specific policy. If you will forgive the brevity of each summary below, the following sections should provide some stimulating food for thought. If you have trouble with an idea, please consider it due to a possible dispective—an incongruity in a label or definition—and not an irreconcilable disagreement. In the end, we all agree on the basic principles that should be promoted in society—as Thomas Jefferson wrote during the founding of his country, the right to life, liberty, and the pursuit of happiness. The only thing that separates us is our perspective on how to attain those rights. I offer here my humble suggestion that the key to attainment is consistency in policy and behavior throughout the world today. I hope you agree.

napoleon dynamite

A decade into the nineteenth century, a man just over five feet tall rose above the entire continent of Europe.[3] In 1812, Napoleon Bonaparte had control of France, Spain, Italy, Prussia (now part of Germany), and Poland, and he held sway with Austria and Russia. His army was a massive collection of troops from around the continent, and it numbered three quarters of a million people. It was this emperor who Chateaubriand dubbed "the mightiest breath of life which ever animated human clay."[4] Napoleon was as ruthless as he was mighty. He didn't care much about the extremely high casualty rate that accompanied his conquests (30 to 40 percent),[5] and his motto was an unrelenting "Toujours l'attaque!" or "Always attack!" In June of 1812, Napoleon was itching for the attack of a lifetime.

Napoleon's army crossed the Niemen River into Russia, breaking a loose treaty between France and the large Eastern power, and began to march toward the capital city of Moscow. Expecting immediate resistance, the army found none at all and marched through the Russian countryside unopposed for months. The country itself proved to be quite a deterrent due to its lack of roads and the scant population to plunder. The Russian forces were retreating toward Moscow; Napoleon's army followed, but his troops were continuously disappointed by the lack of fight. Bonaparte wrote his empress in late June, "The whole Russian force is at [nearby] Vitepsk, we are on the eve of great events."[6] But when the French troops arrived, they found Vitepsk abandoned.

For a military force that had conquered nearly an entire continent, the extended delay to fight their new enemy was wearing. By the time Russia gave its first fight at Smolensk, Napoleon's force had already lost 250,000 deserters (a third of the original army), many of whom were half-hearted conscripts.[7] Napoleon won at Smolensk, but the next fight at Borodino has been considered the bloodiest day in history with 40,000 casualties on each side. There wasn't a clear winner in the battle; the Russians withdrew to their capital and Napoleon pressed on, but the French emperor was clearly shaken by the Borodino battle, calling the Russians "invincible."[8]

When Napoleon arrived in Moscow, ready to defeat the

Russians once and for all, he found the city evacuated and all the foodstuffs taken. A few days later, an order was given by the Russian forces outside of Moscow to burn the city. So, the Russian capital was burned to the ground and Napoleon was left with a troubling question: what does a conqueror do when there's nothing left to conquer? The Russians' scorched earth policy, which entailed destroying everything in Napoleon's path, was giving the French invaders nothing worthwhile to take over, and the defending army was making the French pay at every stop along their devastated countryside. Like a land-fallen hurricane that has lost the fuel it requires to grow and thrive, the once mighty Napoleon was wilting in his lack of conquest. And what the starvation of conquest didn't defeat in Bonaparte's army, the starvation of food did. Deserters, military casualties, and weather- and hunger-related fatalities accounted for the loss of the entire French army except for an unimposing 20,000 troops that staggered over the Niemen River and back to Paris.

The story of the mighty-to-defeated Napoleon is unique in its magnitude but not in its essence. The plot consists of a man who thrives on destruction, and, when there's nothing left to destroy, he himself is defeated. In his novel *Monaco*, Eric Robert Morse wrote succinctly of the Bonaparte disaster in Russia, stating, "Built on the conquered volition of others, when no rival exists, he does not exist."[9]

A behavior that feeds off of the destruction of others (e.g., war) is ultimately self-destructive—it is not consistent with itself and does not perpetuate itself. The more you destroy, the less you *can* destroy. Thus, war is an example of something that is contradictory in nature and bad for itself; and, according to concurrence, that which defeats itself is inherently evil.

A few decades after Napoleon's conquest and back on our continent, Lincoln presided over a unified country for a few days after the end of the Civil War, but that country was completely demoralized and wiped out in every respect. Unlike Lincoln, Napoleon lost his war, and he was left with an even more devastated continent than the U.S. president. But both wars were morally wrong because they were wars of conquest and innately contradictory.

Does that mean, though, that every war is wrong? Aren't there some things worth fighting a war for? The answer to this question is a bit complex, but it can be explained by answering a moral dilemma that we have faced recently. As Kant's universality test showed, it is wrong to kill another person and we all know it intuitively. But what if that someone was going to kill someone else? Would it be morally acceptable for the potential victim to kill in self-defense? Logically speaking, the first priority of a person, a group of people, or a state is to exist. This is so because everything that the person, group, or state does is dependent solely on its existence—for instance, one can't promote an ideology, trade, or thrive if one is dead. And if existence is threatened, it is reasonable for the threatened to use force to defend itself. Killing, in self-defense, then, would be acceptable. So, if a victim is certain the attacker is going to kill him, and the only way to stop him is to beat him to the punch, then the bloody outcome would be morally acceptable according to concurrence. However, we can't foretell the future, and fatal outcomes are never certain. Thus, while killing in self-defense is the only good reason for the act, it can never be fully justified. Applying this to the national level, the first priority of the nation is to exist. War is morally acceptable for a country if it is undeniable that another will destroy it. However, the same qualification applies at this level; we can't predict the future and we can't be sure as to the outcome of any given geopolitical situation; thus, war can never be completely justified.

In the case of the U.S. in WWII, the country did its best to maintain neutrality. But when Pearl Harbor was bombed and further attacks seemed inevitable as German U-boats entered American waters, the U.S. had no choice but to defend itself. Moreover, the U.S. was compelled to come to the aid of its allies (notably Britain and France) whose existence was highly unlikely without U.S. intervention. In this case, war seems reasonable and can be considered moral.

On the other hand, when Iraqi leaders were playing games with the U.S. and kept kicking United Nations officers out of its borders, the safety of the U.S., though not completely clear, was never truly in doubt. Iraq did pose a threat to its neighbors (as it did when it invaded Kuwait a decade earlier), but without much incontrovertible evidence about Iraq's weapons of mass destruction, the self-defense argument does not hold much water (hindsight here is no doubt beneficial). One can make all the rational arguments possible about the benefits of taking out Saddam's regime—Lord knows I have—but the war was not fought on a solid self-defense premise; thus, it was inherently wrong. Let me be clear: good *was* produced from the Iraq war—no longer is a totalitarian, torturous, invading, terrorist-funding maniac sitting on top of a third of the world's oil. But as was the case in the Civil War, right ends do not justify wrong means; there were other ways to achieve our goals. Thus, preemptive wars are never morally acceptable according to concurrence. What the U.S. should do now that it is already in Iraq is another question.

As we have seen with the American Civil War in the last

part and Napoleon's conquests here, war is ultimately contradictory and only understandable if it is fought in self-defense to protect existence, as with America's role in WWII. There may be good reasons for war, as Lincoln found to be true, but a means to an end is never acceptable, even if the end is noble and the means seem inevitable. As another notable president, Dwight Eisenhower, said, "Though force can protect in emergency, only justice, fairness, consideration and cooperation can finally lead men to the dawn of eternal peace."

burn, baby, burn

Out the office door, I look up and see the sun setting. It's a brisk San Diego evening, but I came prepared with a long-sleeve shirt (and how brisk can it get in San Diego?). I stretch for a few minutes, and then I start to jog home. For the better part of a year, this was my evening commute. Accompanied by music and audio books on my iPod, I jogged past hundreds of cars impatiently speeding from red light to red light, spewing exhaust and frustrating their drivers.

I chose to jog home partly because I enjoy running; partly because the four-mile run was quicker on some days than the commute by car; partly because it was better for the environment; and partly because I got a kick out of telling people that I jog to work. Another reason that I decided to commute by foot was the exorbitant cost of fuel. Throughout the year, the average cost of gasoline was about $4.50 a gallon, and, when you add the cost of maintaining a car with oil changes and other checkups, driving became a very expensive practice during that span.

It's no wonder that media outlets talk so dramatically these days about the energy crisis. News reports constantly pound into our psyches the trouble our wallets are already feeling, and energy is getting very expensive—both economically and environmentally. Additionally, while Middle Eastern countries fuel American cars and businesses with oil, we fuel their bank accounts and rarely see that wealth returned except in the form of anti-American propaganda and terrorism. Report after report also tells us that pollution in the air from burning fossil fuels leads to lower life expectancy,[10] not to mention the lower quality of life for people in major metropolitan areas experiencing the smelly haze. Finally, since the Industrial Revolution, advanced societies have been converting a finite amount of fuel into production, and the limited amount we can produce is starting to catch up to our hunger for burning it up.

All of that being said, we're faced with another major moral dilemma—some say the biggest of our generation. Economically, we are forfeiting hundreds of billions of dollars, much of which goes to countries filled with people who don't like us, and some of which is returned to us in the form of attacks on U.S. military bases. Environmentally, we're hurting the ecology that produced us and on which we thrive. In both cases, we're participating in self-destructive behavior—the antithesis of concurrence. As CIA Director Jim Woolsey said in reference to our oil dependence, "We're funding the rope for the hanging of ourselves."[11] Our dilemma is whether to continue on this self-destructive path or move toward more consistent behavior with regard to energy consumption.

Does concurrence offer any sort of insight into the problem, then? Yes, and it doesn't suggest that we all need to stop driving and start jogging to work. First off, I can't condemn the same Industrial Revolution that has allowed me the ability to write about my condemnation—that would be foolish and contradictory. But it's not contradictory to benefit from our past mistakes at the same time as we desist in making them. With regard to concurrence, there are basically two questions to consider in this dilemma: who should pay for developing new, cleaner energies, and what should those energies be? We'll see that the politician-decides-the-rest-of-us-pays method of developing new technology is not the way to go, and that there's one form of energy out there (really a combination of two) that fits all of our changing energy needs and will get us out of the so-called energy crisis.

2008 U.S. presidential candidates John McCain and Barack Obama had some ideas on how to fix the energy crisis, and some of the most popular points during their nomination acceptance speeches were about energy. McCain touted, "We'll attack—we'll attack the problem on every front. We'll produce more energy at home. We will drill new wells off-shore, and we'll drill them now . . . We'll develop clean-coal technology. We'll increase the use of wind, tide, solar, and natural gas. We'll encourage the development and use of flex-fuel, hybrid and electric automobiles."[12] Obama agreed to a vague solution, saying, "As president, as president, I will tap our natural gas reserves, invest in clean coal technology" and "I'll invest $150 billion over the next decade in affordable, renewable sources of energy—wind power, and solar power, and the next generation of biofuels. . . ."[13] From these messages, it seemed that all of our problems would be taken care of as soon as either candidate was sworn in.

But the question is why does government—ultimately, the taxpayer—have to pay for new energy solutions? Energy is an extremely profitable industry. Just look at the lucrative Exxon Mobile Corporation for proof. The oil giant earned a record $11.68 billion in the second quarter of 2008[14]—that's nearly $90,000 a minute during that stretch. Are John McCain and Barack Obama willing to tell us that there's not a company out there willing to cut in on that billionaire ball and do a little clean-energy dance for us? In fact, companies are already trying to get a piece of the action; just look at the ever-growing investment opportunities in alternative energy companies (the companies that broke the initial public offering drought in 2008 were all based in clean-energy technology[15]). Taxpayers don't need to be forced to foot the bill on energy solutions; this idea works against concurrence.

Still, government-mandated solutions have been exalted in the popular media, most recently by Thomas Friedman in his book *Hot, Flat, and Crowded*. Friedman encourages a government-initiated overhaul of the current energy economy, a plan that includes major taxes, investment in renewable energies, and higher regulation. He praises countries like Denmark, which imposed a steep gas tax in the early eighties (the price of gas in Denmark is $9 per gallon) and tacked on a CO_2 tax for energy consumption aside from autos. Friedman notes that Denmark's economy has grown 70 percent since 1981 (370 percent unadjusted for inflation),[16] and the country is poised to lead the way with exportation of clean-energy technologies like wind turbines (Friedman forgot to mention that the U.S. economy has grown at an unadjusted rate of 480 percent in the same time period and leads the world in much more than clean-energy technologies).[17]

We've already seen that investment in renewable energies is necessary for us to be concurrent and avoid slow self-destruction, but Denmark-style government coercion is not the appropriate vehicle for that investment. The U.S. government already tried its hand at forcing green innovation with the Energy Policy Act of 2005. Along with subsidies for wave power, wind energies, and new coal initiatives, the act mandates that an increased amount of ethanol (fuel derived from plants—usually corn) be mixed in with gasoline sold in the U.S. (four billion gallons in 2006).[18] Despite the lawmakers' good intentions, this green initiative has had dire consequences.

There are good things about ethanol, but there are also many reasons why it's not the answer to our energy problem. First off, ethanol is good because it's not a limited resource in the same way that petroleum is—we can grow it and produce fuel from it ourselves. And buying ethanol profits American corn growers, not foreign bank accounts. But ethanol still produces harmful chemicals when burned, reduces fuel efficiency over gasoline, costs more, and the heavy use of ethanol has other non-energy-related side-effects. While burning ethanol causes less greenhouse gas than gasoline, one estimate says that with just half of the Energy Policy mandate, agricultural pollution would increase by 8 percent, negating any improvement in the end use.[19] Also, ethanol is not as efficient as gasoline. A study by *Consumer Reports* showed that a Chevy Tahoe went from fourteen miles per gallon (mpg) on gasoline to ten mpg on ethanol.[20] That loss in efficiency means a higher overall cost of using the biofuel.

Aside from those issues, the large mandated push toward ethanol has created problems in other areas. Since corn has typically gone to our dinner plates instead of our gas tanks, the push for more corn-based fuel has reduced the supply of corn available for food and driven its price up. In 2005, the price of corn was a relatively stable $2 a bushel; it skyrocketed to well over $4 a bushel in 2007.[21] Experts predict the price boom to continue (to nearly $5 a bushel in 2009) as long as the mandate is in place.[22] And we can't just take corn off of our plates to solve the problem. Due to its high fructose corn syrup (HFCS) derivatives and its use as livestock feed, corn is central to much of what we eat; thus the ethanol mandate and subsequent decrease in corn-food supply has affected much more than just the corn crop. Higher corn prices have directly impacted the world market and partially contributed to the skyrocketing prices around the globe that led to riots in places like Haiti and Egypt.[23] With so many unflattering studies and such negative consequences on the world food chain, it's a wonder why government officials insist on forcing such a harmful product on the market—but they do. Ethanol has the sole benefit of reducing our dependence on foreign oil, but are the other consequences worth it?

No. Ethanol isn't the answer to the energy dilemma we face, and, if that's the best solution our government officials have to offer, perhaps government isn't part of the solution either. In fact, it appears that government has been a substantial part of the problem, as we will see shortly.

Many experts in the field say the solution to the energy dilemma is hydrogen, the use of which just happens to be the most morally concurrent. Hydrogen is ubiquitous and local. The most common element in the universe, we don't have to import hydrogen from countries that are filled with America-haters. Hydrogen is also clean. When used for energy, it expels only water vapor as a by-product. Also, hydrogen is about as renewable as energy sources get. If we procure the resource from water (as opposed to cheaper sources like natural gas), the life cycle of the energy is water to hydrogen and back to water—transforming some of the mass into energy. Moreover, we already have the technology to produce hydrogen and use it to become a truly hydrogen-based economy. In the auto arena, Honda has been the first out of the gate with a lease-only model, the Honda Clarity, for customers in Southern California. The Chevy Equinox is also on the road in test markets. Both hydrogen-powered cars release no carbon emissions and are nearly three times as efficient as gas-powered vehicles for the same amount of fuel.

If hydrogen is so perfect, then why haven't we completely dived into the hydrogen pool? There are a number of reasons, but one is more insidious than the rest. One reason is that researchers are still looking for ideal ways to produce and distribute the energy source. Like other energy sources, including petroleum and natural gas, usable hydrogen isn't available naturally—it needs to be produced from a specific resource. Hydrogen must be extracted from water (or from natural gas) to be used as a clean energy, a process that takes energy in itself.[24] Many have proposed that geothermal and hydroelectric power be used to create the hydrogen needed for other energy uses, but those sources aren't sufficient enough (together they account for under 5 percent of all U.S. energy production and are practically maxed out at current technology levels).[25] Solar and wind power are great clean energies, but they are limited and inconsistent and cannot be counted on to support the world's energy needs. Some scientists have gone so far as to say that large-scale expansion of these energies would be horrible for the amount of land and development they would require to sustain our economy. Conservation biologist and climate change researcher Jesse Ausubel refers to wind and solar energy as "boutique fuels," saying, "They look attractive when they are quite small. But if we start producing renewable energy on a large scale, the fallout is going to be horrible." To match the output of an average nuclear reactor (1,000 megawatts), we'd have to cover 150 square miles of photovoltaic solar cells, or the entire state of Texas (268,000 square miles), with wind turbines.[26]

Nuclear energy, on the other hand, is extremely consistent, efficient, and far safer than any fossil fuel on the market. Nuclear plants do have a minimal risk of meltdown (as in the Chernobyl and Three Mile Island accidents), but the deaths from those mishaps (about 1,000) pale in comparison to the tens of thousands of deaths each year associated with coal production (China reported over 6,000 coal mining deaths in 2004 alone) and consumption.[27] Current safety standards have been effective in eliminating deaths in the procurement of nuclear energy. While nuclear plants do produce waste, this waste can be contained, unlike the pollution and waste produced by coal plants or petroleum (which together provide the U.S. with 84 percent of its energy).[28] Some countries already take full advantage of nuclear energy as a relatively clean and efficient energy source. France, for instance, leads the way in nuclear usage; nearly 80 percent of the country's energy comes from its nuclear plants.[29] But on our side of the pond, the U.S. government has restricted nuclear development because of its fear of misguided environmentalists and the special interest groups that represent competing energy sources like petroleum.

Government intervention plays an unfortunate role in the resistance to a hydrogen-focused economy. The merits of the hydrogen/nuclear combo would easily outweigh those of other energies, but special interests (mainly biofuel farmers) have pushed federal policy in an unhealthy direction and practically forced less desirable energy solutions, like ethanol, on us. The reason is simple; lobbyists can target a few policy-making politicians relatively easily, but for special interests to persuade an entire country of consumers, their argument needs to be a lot more convincing. We don't need an artificial push toward government mistakes, and (sorry, Mr. Friedman) we don't need a $10-a-gallon tax on gas to pay for those mistakes.

What we *can* do—and what is most concurrent—is invest in companies that are developing hydrogen technologies and applying them to transportation (I don't want to list specific stock tips here, but a simple Google search will come up with a number of companies that are making great strides in the field). We can also vote for politicians who promise to cut restrictions on new nuclear plants and those who cut regulations and mandates on other forms of energy. The energy problem is too big for a few hundred people in Washington to decide for us. Everyone needs to participate in finding the solution. If that happens, I'll probably still be jogging home from work, but I won't *have* to.

life and death

The photo album looked years old but was still well-preserved and in decent shape. And it had been taken care of for good reason, too; it was full of pictures of adorable children and promising young adults, all of whom owed something profound to the book's owner. Mixed in with pictures of Bridgets and Michaels throughout the album were notes from the children themselves and from their parents thanking the album's owner profusely. Most of the notes went something like, "Thank you for saving my life! I'm studying to become a nurse now to help others." In fact, the owner of the book had saved—count 'em—205 lives as documented by the powerful photo album.[30] But the owner of the book isn't a medical doctor who performed miracle heart transplants on young children; nor is the owner a firefighter who specializes in rescuing children from burning buildings. She is a sidewalk counselor who offers support to women considering abortion; the 205 children and young adults in the book were saved from termination while they were in their mothers' wombs.

Geri, the sidewalk counselor and owner of the photo album, has been offering support to women entering abortion clinics for twenty-four years, and the response she's experienced has been overwhelming. One mother calls Geri regularly and thanks her for saving her baby (the mother's fourth child). Another mom, whose son is now twenty-one years old, says that she will always trust Geri because Geri always tells her the truth. Another mother explained that Geri "saved four people the day you spoke to me about my baby." Doctors had warned her of fetal abnormalities and said her baby would be born physically disabled. As a result, her husband had pressured her to have an abortion because, as he put it, it was wrong to bring a baby with defects into this world. The pregnant mother reasoned that, had she gone through with the abortion, she would have resented her husband and blamed him for the loss of their child. She figured they would have gotten a divorce, which would have ruined their other child's life, as well as both of theirs. Geri helped to convince the mother to carry her child to term and, as it turned out, the baby was born without the forewarned physical defects. The father was relieved, the family stayed together, and four lives were *saved* as a result of one person's thoughtful deeds.

Of course, not all stories involving sidewalk counseling have the fairytale endings like the stories above. Much of the reaction sidewalk counselors receive when they approach would-be abortion patients is cold and disinterested or antagonistic and highly defensive. If they are not completely ignored, the counselors are yelled at and sometimes physically assaulted in reaction to their pleas for life. This behavior is certainly understandable; after all, the woman about to have an abortion is doing the right thing in her mind (and her partner's mind), and she believes the counselors are attempting to take away her *right* to have an abortion.

Moreover, the counselors are often linked—subconsciously if in no other way—to anti-abortion activists who go so far as to commit barbaric crimes to counter the perceived evil of abortion. One such activist, James Kopp, shot a prominent New York abortion doctor in his home in 1998.[31] The killing was rightly received with outrage as the governor at the time, George Pataki, said, "It's beyond a tragedy. It's really an act of terrorism and, in my mind, a cold-blooded assassination." President Clinton said, "All Americans must stand together in condemning this tragic and brutal act." Another official familiar with the incident said, "For anyone to take it upon himself to be judge, jury and executioner is nothing but sheer evil." The disgust and condemnation of such an act is absolutely warranted, but the context of the barbaric slaying begs the question: how can people condemn one killing and at the same time support, and even fight for, over 1.2 million killings each year in the United States—those of unborn children?[32]

The answer is obvious; those pregnant women and their partners entering an abortion clinic don't think that an unborn child, especially in the early stages of growth, constitutes a living human. Their opponents in the debate, on the other hand, believe the embryo and fetus do constitute human life. Thus, the abortion argument boils down to a simple dispective—people on one side of the disagreement see abortion as killing, and people on the other side view abortion as terminating a trivial collection of cells. The dispective is inflated when the participants in the debate label themselves. One side is *pro-choice* and the other is *pro-life*, insinuating that the opposition is *anti-choice* or *anti-life*. When two sides of a dispective polarize into an us-against-them paradigm, people start lumping together acts of goodness like sidewalk counseling and vile crimes like doctor assassination, and truth is compromised.

From a dispassionate standpoint, the abortion debate appears to be one of those morally gray arguments in which there is no clear right or wrong (on one side people fight for life; on the other side, people fight for liberty). Why else would so many people be so ardently in favor of opposing views? But as we've seen with other moral dilemmas, when the abortion debate is analyzed in the framework of concurrence, a moral solution becomes apparent, though it may not be quite the solution you're expecting. Everyone involved in the abortion debate should be able to agree on two basic principles: life is valuable, and liberty is valuable. So, when you get down to it, both sides in the debate are right—women should be allowed to do what they deem appropriate with their own bodies (the pro-choice stance) *and* human life should be respected and preserved at all stages (the pro-life stance). Like many other moral dilemmas, abortion has two strong cases, yet only one is completely consistent with itself and, thus, morally acceptable.

If we can agree that everyone has an unalienable right to do whatever he or she wants as long as it doesn't harm someone else and that everyone has an innate right to life, the only factor in question in the abortion debate, then, is whether the unborn baby is an actual "someone else." Many readers may have a hard time being open to this concept, but the only consistent position with regard to abortion is that human life starts at conception and, if it is wrong to kill a postnatal human, concurrence necessitates that it is wrong to abort a prenatal human. The main point of dissent in the argument appears to be what constitutes a human life, so we will work backwards from birth to conception and compare the prenatal being with the postnatal being to apply concurrence to the heated debate.

It is generally accepted in the United States and every other civilized culture that killing a human baby after birth (the procedure called infanticide) is wrong, even if she is just one day old. There are major differences between a baby that has been born and one that is still inside the womb (the source of nutrients and oxygen, for example), but there are many more similarities. The prenatal baby still feels, thinks, and emotes just like a one-day-old. In addition, the one-day-old is no more self-sufficient than the one-day-prenatal baby; she requires just as much care, or more, than an unborn baby. Before the baby is born, the mother feeds and warms the baby involuntarily; but after birth, the baby requires feeding and clothing and clean-up for her little messes. However, there's very little physically or mentally different from a prenatal baby and a one-day-old. So, to be consistent, if one considers infanticide immoral, one must also consider abortion (at least late-term abortion) immoral.

But abortion advocates don't usually promote late-term abortion (those committed in the last third of a natural pregnancy). Instead, some abortion advocates condone early-term abortions on the grounds that the embryo doesn't feel in the same sense that we adult humans feel. If abortion were painful, then it would be immoral, they may concede. But while most legal abortions occur in the first trimester of gestation, practically no doctor-administered abortions happen before the embryo has begun to develop a nervous system, which starts on the eighteenth day after conception.[33] Many abortion advocates claim that, at this primitive stage, embryos don't feel anything (some also claim that babies don't feel until after they're born). All we can know for sure, however, is what organs fetuses have, and nearly all abortions are committed after the fetus has already developed a spinal cord, a brain, and a heart.[34]

Other abortion advocates emphasize transition points that represent the shift from embryo or fetus to human being (i.e., when an embryo loses the gills or tail or when the fetus begins to "look" human). This reasoning has its merits; after all, embryos look more like something out of a sci-fi flick than a human photo album. So what, according to abortion advocates, are the distinctions between an embryo, a fetus, and a *more human* human? They are physiological—facial structure, placement of eyes, lips, nose, and a developed body (i.e., one without a tail).

To be sure, a fetus doesn't look much like one of us adults, But by the abortion advocate's rationale, we're not conceived as humans; we transition into humans at some point during gestation. It's clear, though, that we humans are constantly changing our appearance, and still we are no less human throughout the process. Does it make sense to say that because a one-day-old baby doesn't *look* like an adult, she isn't a human, or because a child can't do some of the physiological things an adult can do, he doesn't have a right to life? Do the physical changes caused by old age make the elderly any less human? Further, does physical damage (picture a poor guy who survived a fire with substantial burn injuries) mean that a person isn't human anymore? No. We don't change from inhuman to human and back again due to our appearance—we're always human. This is because a human life is not defined by one's appearance or functionality; a human life is defined by one's genes, which are, with little exception, consistent from the time a human looks like a little Sea-Monkey, to the day she is born, to the time she is old enough to take a picture for Geri's photo album. Our individual genome, the unique collection of genes that contains our entire lifecycle in a few megabytes of data, makes us who we are and gives us value within our species. In other words, it's not our appearance that makes us human but our DNA (a stipulation on which the Human Genome Project to define the basis of human life centered its thirteen-year research).[35]

It's true that there are millions of unwanted pregnancies each year, and I don't envy the tortured souls who must go through with an unplanned pregnancy or have an abortion. But, unfortunately, there are unwanted postnatal children in this society, too; should their parents be allowed to terminate them as well? To be consistent, if someone accepts the act of abortion on the grounds of *unwanted* life, he or she necessarily condones the killing of unwanted postnatal children, too. But murder is wrong and we as a civilization must realize the contradictory nature of disapproving murder yet approving abortion, and we must acknowledge the gravity of moral implications from that contradiction. One can discount the value of life itself to support abortion, but if one considers killing a baby wrong, consistency requires abortion to be condemned as well.

A common argument in favor of abortion draws upon instances in which there is a potential for abnormalities in the unborn child. Geri, the sidewalk counselor mentioned earlier, relayed to me the story of a pregnant mother who was considering an abortion after her prenatal child was diagnosed with Down syndrome, a chromosomal disorder which results in substantial cognitive and physical impairment. As a friend of the pregnant woman said, no one wants a Down baby. The pregnant woman gave Geri three days to find an adoptive family or else she would go through with the abortion. Geri responded, "Piece of cake."

Geri spread the word, and, through the help of several Internet-based programs, she received over six hundred emails from people interested in adopting the baby. "Our dad just lost his job," one respondent proclaimed, "but we will pull together and adopt this baby." Another said, "We have Downs kids and want to tell that Mom that she will LOVE her baby." The pregnant woman was skeptical when Geri told her the good news. "Do they know that the baby will be black?" she said. Geri relayed the new information to the potential families, and the response was overwhelming—they wanted the baby regardless of skin color. One claimed, "If the baby is green with spots, we still want [him]." Granted, this is just one instance, but with the documented growing popularity of Down adoptions,[36] it's evident that there is a wealth of support for life, even in more trying situations.

Of course, a respect for life should be universal and that means that the anti-abortion activists who choose to murder abortion doctors are guilty of moral contradiction as well. As established above, killing, even to save a life, is contradictory and morally unacceptable. The anti-abortion activists would claim that there is a difference between the unborn child and an abortion doctor, and they are right. The unborn child is absolutely innocent of any wrongdoing and the abortion doctor, in their eyes, has committed a moral evil. But applying evil to more evil does not create good; as the aphorism goes, "two wrongs don't make a right."

That saying also pertains to people who have been tried in a criminal court as much as to abortion doctors tried only by a lone activist. Thus, to be consistent with regard to human life, we must acknowledge that the death penalty is also contradictory in a society that supposedly values life. The premise—killing someone to teach that killing is wrong—just doesn't make sense. Sure, we want to expel vicious criminals from our society, and prison in that regard is warranted. But a death row inmate has already been expelled from society for the rest of his life; killing him simply reduces the executioner to criminal status along with the prisoner.

Admittedly, there are some benefits to the death penalty. For instance, some degree of vengeance is enacted with a death sentence, and society does save money on prison expenses through execution. But a crime cannot be undone, and death sentences aren't cheap. Studies show that death penalty trials cost 40 to 70 percent more than non-death penalty trials, not including the actual cost of execution.[37] Additionally, the justice system is not perfect, and innocent people are imprisoned and die at the hand of the state annually—an unacceptable consequence of state-authorized killing. As proof of the imperfect justice system, exonerations of death row inmates continue to climb (one study has the count at 130 exonerations as of the date of this writing),[38] showing that by no means is everyone sentenced to death guilty.

At the same time, prisons should not be Disneyland for criminals. It would be morally wrong to support prison facilities that promote more criminal behavior if and when criminals leave. If the death penalty is wiped out as a deterrent, it must be clear that those who harm others will be punished accordingly.

The call to action here is simple and attainable. We must demand the cessation of federal funding of the death penalty and of corporations that provide abortion services. Without federal funding, states will be forced to decide whether these acts are right or wrong, and citizens will be able to choose which states they want to associate with—those that support barbaric and morally contradictory killing or those that choose to be morally consistent in their respect for life. There is value in all life, and only when we acknowledge that will we be able to truly live ourselves.

let freedom reign

One of the largest financial crises since the Great Depression struck the United States in late 2008, and a lot of peculiar things were said and done about it. One aspect of this crisis stands out to me more than any other. In the 1930s, we had a president who told us to calm down, stating, "The only thing we have to fear is fear itself."[39] During the 2008 financial meltdown, on the other hand, we had a president who tried to scare us with comments like, "our country could experience a long and painful recession"[40] and "this sucker could go down,"[41] meaning the entire economy. If the situation was as dire as President Bush made it seem, why did he need to resort to such scare tactics?

The answer is simple. President Bush wanted us to fear an economic meltdown so much that we wouldn't question the bill he proposed, which would have given the Treasury Secretary seemingly unrestricted control over one-thirteenth of the U.S. economy (the infamous Wall Street bailout bill euphemized as the Troubled Asset Relief Program). And with the help of the largest single-day stock market decline ever right after the House of Representatives rejected the bill, the fear of a financial catastrophe was ingrained even more. Eventually, Bush and Treasury Secretary Henry Paulson got their $700 billion bailout bill approved by both the Senate and the House. Not coincidentally, however, the stock markets reacted to the bill's passing much more negatively than to its rejection (the Dow Jones Industrial Average dropped nearly 20 percent in the five-day span after Congress *approved* the bailout plan).

The bailout plan was just part of a major push by politicians in the federal government to regulate and oversee the free market in order to stabilize it. As the president said in an address to the nation, "Once this crisis is resolved, there will be time to update our financial regulatory structures." In a vague description of those structures, he equivocated, "For example, the Federal Reserve would be authorized to take a closer look at the operations of companies across the financial spectrum and ensure that their practices do not threaten overall financial stability."[42] Not surprisingly, while the opposition Democrats continuously slammed Republican President Bush about "failed policy," they agreed with Bush about the need for more regulation policy. Democratic U.S. Congressman Barney Frank of Massachusetts, Chairman of the House Financial Services Committee throughout the crisis and its buildup, wholeheartedly believed in regulation as the solution to the financial mess. He told a reporter that the problem in the financial sector was "lack of regulation" and that "we believe what you have to do is put regulations in place to prevent this from happening again."[43]

This debate on the financial crisis has brought to the forefront the question of freedom in general. Is there such a thing as too much freedom with regard to financial behavior or otherwise? From the quotes of Bush and Frank, it appears that some people believe freedom can get out of hand, especially when an entire economy is on the line. As one *LA Times* article declared, "Politicians and experts are now looking with favor at more, not less, government involvement [less freedom] in the economy."[44]

But as we'll see using the theory of concurrence, the bipartisan support to increase government regulation is not such a hot idea as everyone seems to be making it out to be. Freedom is at stake here—the freedom to do what we want as long as it doesn't hurt others. Some government officials think they can protect our economy by restricting freedoms, but that idea is diametrically illogical and contrary to the idea of concurrence. The problem lies in a misunderstanding. Bush and Frank's push for more government regulation is based on the premise that free markets created the financial crisis, but, as we'll see, that premise is completely misguided; freedom didn't create the economic crisis—*lack* of freedom did.

The first thing we should address when tackling the philosophical behemoth of freedom in the marketplace is the concept of freedom itself. When we are faced with questions about what caused the mortgage crisis or who's to blame for failed banks, we must first revisit the topic described in Part IV: free will. As human beings, do we even have free will in the first place and do we have the power to make our own choices? These are questions that have confounded philosophers, neuroscientists, and politicians alike, but as of yet have no definitive answers. It's no wonder, then, that philosopher David Hume called the issue of free will "the most contentious question of metaphysics."[45]

The difficulty with the concept of free will is in a seeming paradox in our collective knowledge. We feel as though we have the freedom to do what we want and to change our environment, but science consistently shows us that we live in a deterministic world and that, in all likelihood, we have no control over our universe or even our behavior. For example, pick an action—smiling, jumping up and down, whatever—and do it now. Whether you decided to act or not, you probably felt like you had control in the matter. You made a decision and acted (or refused to act in defiance of my humble request). That's free will. On the other side of the debate there is deterministic physics, which says that every act—even human behavior—is a result of the preceding state of affairs. This alternative to free will suggests that, sure, you felt like you decided to act (or not act) just now, but the act was suggested by the words in this book, and the act itself was derived from your experience and your preset desires. The decision to act was based on a mechanical evaluation of whether you could act and whether doing so would be beneficial.

The free will debate is extensive and timeless and can only be given its appropriate due in another volume (see Book III of *Everyone Agrees*). Still, the question of free will drastically impacts the entire concept of morality, and we must take a position on it one way or the other for a discussion about morality to have any value. After all, if you have absolutely no choice in what you do, you can't really do right or wrong. With choice, we can say things *ought* to be a certain way; without choice, things just are. To demonstrate this, I will employ a thought experiment.

Each moral decision we make will have good or bad consequences regardless of free will, but right and wrong can only exist in a world that includes free will. For instance, taking someone else's slice of blackberry pie is always good for me and my taste buds and bad for the previous owner who won't be able to enjoy it. But if I can choose whether to leave it or steal it and deprive the rightful owner of the slice of yumminess, the question becomes a moral dilemma: should I entertain my taste buds or preserve self-evident property rights? If I don't have free will and I can't control my behavior—whether consciously or subconsciously—there is no sense in calling my act right or wrong; it just is. And since a book about morality would be pretty pointless if we didn't actually have the ability to choose right or wrong, I will take inventor Isaac Singer's view on the topic: "We have to believe in free will. We've got no choice."[46] For our purposes here, we must assume that we have free will.

If we can at least stipulate that we have free will, we can apply the concept of concurrence to it: a free act is good if and only if it agrees with itself and thus promotes more free acts; whereas a free act is bad if it contradicts itself and consequently limits other free acts. If we can also agree that free will—at least at the level of our cognitive ability—is unique to humanity and is what differentiates us from other species, then one of the ultimate manifestations of the theory of concurrence as it relates to humanity is as follows: liberty is human and coercion is inhuman. This applies to everyday activities, like deciding what to eat for dinner, as well as monumental governmental decisions, like determining whether taxpayers should pay for failed banks.

As humans, liberty is important to us, and we strive for it constantly in our daily lives. Children fight to wear what they want to school, adults vote for various rights, and everyone wants more options for their car or cell phone; in essence, we are a species that treasures—even requires—our freedoms. As you may remember, both the atheist Hitchens and the Christian D'Souza saw their distinct belief systems as the path to the shared value of liberty. Likewise, the Democratic candidate who promotes social welfare programs and the Republican who fights for lower taxes both want the same thing—liberty—albeit in different forms. The Democrat wants the underprivileged to be free to live the American dream, and the Republican wants hardworking Americans to be able to continue living the American dream. Lincoln wanted liberty for the slaves, and Southerners wanted it for themselves. Manufacturers want the freedom to produce what they want, and environmentalists want freedom from pollution. In addition, pro-choice advocates want liberty for women, and pro-life advocates want it for unborn children. In short, liberty is more than just a nice ideal; it's something that everyone can agree on. And to be truly concurrent, we must value liberty for everyone, not just for ourselves.

There's a good reason we all agree on and strive for liberty, too. When we achieve liberty in the form of increased rights and options, we're healthier. Studies have shown that increased liberty (even if the increase is only perceived) lowers anxiety and increases confidence.[47] Sabina Alkire of the Oxford Poverty and Human Development Institute said in an interview, "People's ability to be an agent, to act on behalf of what matters to them, is fundamental."[48] And not only are freedom and liberty good for our state of mind, they may also help us to live longer.

The importance of liberty as an integral part of life was revealed dramatically in one study conducted at a nursing home. Researchers had a hunch that the poor quality of life in institutional settings like retirement homes was at least in part due to the fact that nursing-home life was decision-less—the residents had no opportunity to apply free will—as they could not make decisions like what to eat, where to travel, or whom to meet. The researchers gave residents one plant each, telling half the residents that their plants were their responsibility and that they could decide how to care for them, while telling the other half that a nurse would take care of their plants. After six months, the results of the study showed a clear difference. The residents who were able to choose how to care for their plants (the ones who had more liberty) were much happier and, quite literally, much more alive. The average death rate at the home was 25 percent before the experiment, but only 15 percent of the residents who were able to make choices concerning their plants' well-being died during the study. On the other hand, 30 percent of the residents who had no plant responsibility died during the same time period.[49] Liberty without life is necessarily nonexistent, but, as this study shows, life without liberty is pretty unappealing as well.

If the link between life and liberty is so strong, though, one would expect to see some sort of proof of the connection on a large scale—and one would be right. Freedom House is a nonprofit, nonpartisan organization that publishes an annual evaluation of each country with respect to its political and civil liberties. According to Freedom House, a free country allows its citizens to vote in legitimate elections for officials who are accountable to their constituents, and it allows freedom of expression, belief, and personal autonomy. I compared the rankings Freedom House gave to a number of countries with the life expectancy rates attributed to those countries and found a clear trend. The freest countries generally have the highest life expectancy, and the least free have the lowest.[50]

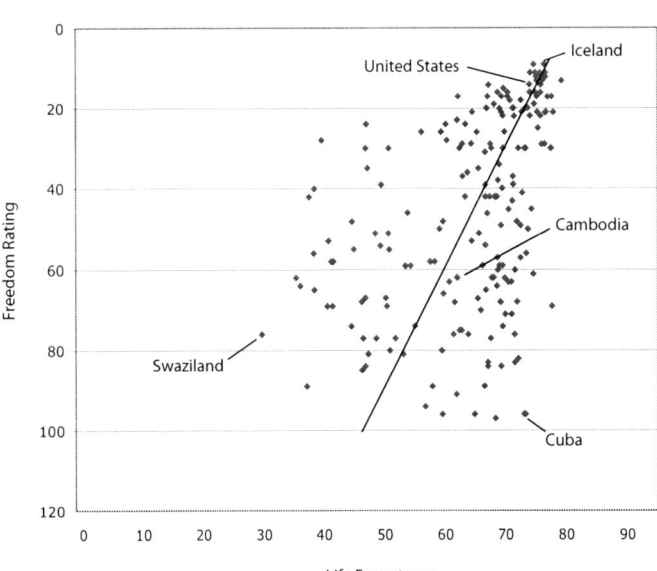

Fig. 12. Countries with higher freedom ratings tend to have longer life expectancy.

The Heritage Foundation is another nonprofit that produces an index of the world's countries according to freedom, specifically economic freedom. According to Heritage, a completely free country consists of "an absolute right of property ownership, fully realized freedoms of movement for labor, capital, and goods, and an absolute absence of coercion or constraint of economic liberty beyond the extent necessary for citizens to protect and maintain liberty itself."[51] When compared with life expectancy, this data provided an even clearer picture of the link between life and liberty.

The act of killing has been condemned by cultures since

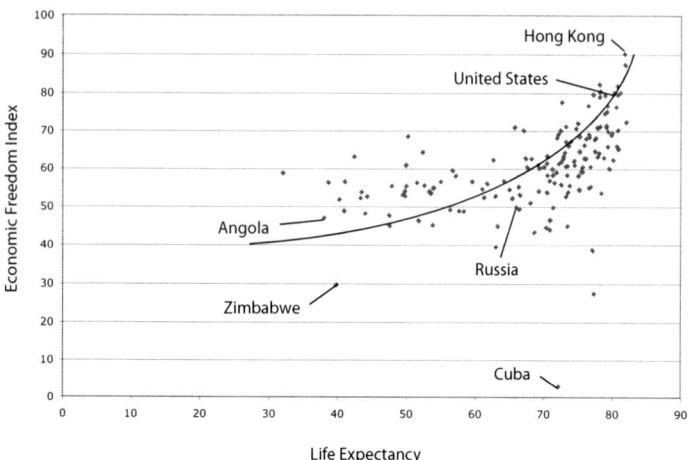

Fig. 13. Countries with higher economic freedom tend to have longer life expectancy as well.

well before Moses brought down the first edition of the Ten Commandments, almost as if opposition to the act is hard-wired into our brains. However, proving that the restriction of liberty is on par with killing is another story. Most people think that a little regulation here or a few more taxes there is okay and that restriction of liberty in general is a worthwhile price for whatever important end it serves. But as the retirement home studies show, and what the hard data from Freedom House, The Heritage Foundation, and the CIA indicate, is that freedom is integral to the life of a being with free will, and the restriction of that freedom is tantamount to a slow death.

The practical upshot of this connection is simple and vitally important to us in the midst of a political climate that seems to continuously erode the inherent liberties that are integral to our life expectancy. We, as a collective population, need to promote government that grants to its constituents more liberty and fewer restrictions. This means less economic coercion (through taxes), more civil liberties, less regulation, fewer laws in general, and fewer government mandates (like the ethanol mistake mentioned above). Promotion of liberty also means that we need to guard against government takeovers of large banks and trillion-dollar bailouts of Wall Street firms.

These aren't new propositions; some brilliant people thought of them over two hundred years ago when they created the United States of America. Thomas Jefferson wrote it down in a straightforward manner when he spoke for the nascent country in 1776, using the words, "We hold these truths to be self-evident: that all men are created equal; that they are endowed by their Creator with certain unalienable Rights; that among these are Life, Liberty and the pursuit of Happiness."[52] To many, it may sound kitschy to quote such a cliché in a world that has generally accepted the role of an overbearing government, but I would rather be a naïve free man than a know-it-all slave. Jefferson's words are as profound today as they were when they were written, and they are now even more necessary as a moral guidepost. We don't need 70,000 pages of the Federal Register[53] to tell us what to do, how to do it, and when; all we need are Jefferson's prescient words.

Despite the Founding Fathers' stand for justice, the government they created has slowly moved away from their ideal. Government is just like any living thing—it wants to survive and grow, and it will, as a collective unit, naturally do everything in its power to expand its reach and breadth. But government isn't self-sufficient; it requires a populace to support it and to allow it to survive and grow. Consequently, the more government expands, the more it harms the constituents it was chartered to protect, thus contradicting its own expansion. The central problem with the contradictory nature of government is that there are far too many people whose primary occupation involves using their free will to limit the liberty of others.

Yes, people have good intentions when they pass laws that take money from one population, take a percentage for themselves, and give the rest to a supposedly needier population. Yes, politicians mean well when they tell us that they are taking away some liberties to protect us. And yes, their hearts are in the right place when they use the American taxpayer as an insurance policy for large financial meltdowns. But, as we saw in the previous part, good ends don't justify evil means; and taking money from and limiting the freedoms of an entire population is contradictory and, thus, morally unacceptable. Like any large organization, government is full of self-interested people that want to ensure their jobs and help their employer grow in size. The only difference is that government officials can force other citizens to do their will through taxation or regulation whereas everyday corporations cannot. Thus, a government that oversteps its charter to protect liberty can rightly be labeled as a threat to that liberty.

It's clear to most Americans that government has overstepped its charter, specifically with the 2008 bailout package. Most Americans opposed Bush's $700 billion corporate welfare plan and practically everyone involved in the legislation of the package agreed that it wasn't ideal. Even those who said we needed to pass the bill admitted its flaws. President Bush, a self-proclaimed supporter of free enterprise, said that his "natural instinct is to oppose government intervention. I believe companies that make bad decisions should be allowed to go out of business." In other words, he wouldn't have promoted the bailout package under normal circumstances. Democratic Congressman Frank agreed that the bailout was a bad move, saying, "We just had to pass a bill that no one was happy to pass." But under the circumstances leading up to the credit crisis, these politicians felt it was necessary to regulate. After all, they thought, it was the lack of regulation that led to the crisis in the first place.

But what *was* the real cause of the financial crisis? It turns out that unfettered free markets weren't the problem that caused the financial crisis, government intervention was. In 1999, the government-chartered company Fannie Mae, which bought loans from home mortgage companies and resold them as securities, received pressure from the outgoing Clinton administration to ease its credit requirements for home mortgages. As a result, the new CEO of Fannie Mae, Harold Raines, changed the course of the mortgage giant to emphasize affordable rental housing and home ownership for less qualified buyers. As Raines said, "Fannie Mae has expanded home ownership for millions of families in the 1990s by reducing down payment requirements."[56] And, backed by the U.S. taxpayer, Fannie Mae had a lot more power than other mortgage companies in order to offer less qualified loans. By 2001, Fannie controlled 43 percent of the mortgage market.[57]

The inevitable result was that mortgage companies sold loans to buyers they knew could not afford to pay back those loans. Why? Because government-backed Fannie Mae was eager to take the loans off the hands of the banks. The situation was compounded when, in 2004, the U.S. Department of Housing and Urban Development required Fannie Mae (and its partner Freddie Mac) to purchase even more "affordable" loans from banks.[58] Backed by the American taxpayer, government officials increased the amount of bad loans on the books to problematic levels.

The intent of this government intrusion into the free market was good; the Clinton and Bush administrations wanted more people to own a home and enjoy a larger slice of the American pie. However, it's clear that their policy was misguided. Allowing more people to purchase homes increased the demand, which—no surprise—made home prices skyrocket. The government's policies blew the housing bubble that saw 20-plus percent gains in home values year after year from 2004 to 2007, making it more difficult for everyone to buy a home. In addition, government policies saddled banks and mortgage companies with trillions of dollars in risky debt that became "toxic" debt once the housing and credit markets began to tighten up when the bubble burst. The mortgage market was plugging along just fine for decades before government policy beginning in the late nineties increased sub-prime lending in an unsustainable way.

Thus, it is reasonable to conclude that irresponsible government intervention in the free market, not the free market itself, caused the financial debacle in the last half of 2008. As the *New York Times* writer Steven A. Holmes predicted in an article in 1999 about the risky government intervention, "In moving, even tentatively, into this new area of lending, Fannie Mae is taking on significantly more risk, which may not pose any difficulties during flush economic times. But the government-subsidized corporation may run into trouble in an economic downturn, prompting a government rescue similar to that of the savings and loan industry in the 1980s."[59] Regrettably, that's exactly what happened. And Bush and Frank's plan to make innocent people pay for the mistakes of government officials was the inevitable cost of careless legislation. In fact, those politicians, along with many others, are trying to fix the financial crisis by applying the same techniques (taxpayer-backed bailouts) that got us in to the mess in the first place.

Seeing that unwarranted government intervention into the free markets set us up for the financial crisis in 2008, it's only reasonable to conclude that more of the same isn't going to get us out of the mess. The only thing that will get us on solid footing is a return to sound fiscal policies and a return to the small-government mentality that the United States was founded on. This will take an enormous paradigm shift in the public mindset, but I believe that it's in everyone's best interest. After all, liberty is something that everyone can agree on.

If we can agree that free will is inherent to humanity, perhaps we can also agree that the most concurrent, and consequently the most moral, manifestation of that free will is the promotion of liberty. Also, life and liberty are inherently intertwined. As Thomas Jefferson said, "The God who gave us life gave us liberty at the same time; the hand of force may destroy, but cannot disjoin them."[60] Without liberty, we can never be truly alive. We all know this to be true whether we're conscious of it or not, and, as a result, we strive toward our own personal liberty. But to be moral is to be consistent, and we need to promote freedom everywhere for everyone, not just in our own lives. We need to limit coercion by the government just as we seek to limit unwanted force by private enterprise or by individual citizens. After all, to quote Benjamin Franklin, "Any society that would give up a little liberty to gain a little security will deserve neither and lose both."[61]

onward

In 1933, the German Student Association's Main Office for Press and Propaganda (yes, they had an office for that) started a campaign to cleanse the literary world of so-called un-German literary works. The campaign climaxed in nationwide parades that ended with bonfires of burning books, a seemingly joyous celebration to the tune of marching bands, fire oaths, and incantations.[62] The ceremonies continued after the initial censorship campaign fizzled out; one estimate puts the total number of books burned in Nazi Germany and occupied territories at one hundred million. But that type of celebration couldn't last. A society that thrives off of the destruction of opposing knowledge necessarily loses steam after all the opposing knowledge has gone up in flames. Once they've finished destroying the opposition, they must either broaden their scope of destruction to keep up the fervor or lose it entirely. Just like the Napoleonic conquest, book burning is an ultimately self-destructive activity, as summed up perfectly in a quote on a recent music album by the band Stars, which says, "When there's nothing left to burn, you have to set yourself on fire."[63]

In a startling and horrific way, the Nazis did just that. Years after the book burning, in 1938, Adolf Hitler approved the first Gnadentod, or "mercy death," of a blind infant who was born with one leg and part of an arm missing.[64] The German Chancellor ordered his doctor, Karl Brandt, to inspect the hospitalized infant and, if the reports of deformity he had received were correct, to carry out the euthanasia. Brandt reported that the doctors on staff at the hospital were of the opinion that "there was no justification for keeping [such a child] alive." So, the child was terminated. Brandt later claimed that Hitler wanted the procedure to be understood as a reasonable medical practice in such situations, saying, "the parents should not have the impression that they themselves were responsible for the death." Brandt returned to Berlin after the procedure to begin an official Nazi program to carry out similar mercy killings in comparable medical situations.

As Robert Jay Lifton wrote in his insightful book, *The Nazi Doctors*, that first mercy killing was a pivotal "test case" for two future programs of Nazi barbarism, the killing of deformed children and the killing of mentally ill adult patients. In one program, physicians documented newborn babies and children up to the age of three according to their health (deformities, idiocy, or other conditions) and their family history (including heavy use of alcohol or nicotine). This information was passed on to a board in the authoritative-sounding Reich Committee for the Scientific Registration of Serious Hereditary and Congenital Diseases, which decided whether to "treat" (i.e., kill) the patient or let the child live. In just a few years, over five thousand children were killed in the Nazi program,[65] and, though Hitler officially terminated the program in 1941, it is widely believed that the killing of children continued—perhaps even increased—afterward.

Before he ended the child euthanasia program, Hitler expanded it to adults. Incurable mentally ill individuals, or those who were simply "not employable or [were] employable only in simple mechanical work," were evaluated for possible euthanasia. Those whom the Nazi doctors recommended for "treatment" were shipped off to aptly termed "killing centers," in which mass murder of the patients was committed. In all, the adult euthanasia program claimed over seventy thousand lives.[66] What was the method of choice for the euthanasia of patients who were considered "life unworthy of life" by some in the Third Reich? The gas chamber, the contraption that was widely used later when the definition of "life unworthy of life" came to include Jews, Catholics, Africans, Gypsies, Poles, Russian prisoners of war, homosexuals, Jehovah's Witnesses, and some Eastern European intellectuals as they were herded into concentration camps and sentenced to death.[67] What started as so-called responsible mercy killings eventually turned into a horrific attempt at mass genocide in the paradoxical "killing to heal" programs. And once the Nazis got the taste of blood, the killing snowballed; reports number the total deaths at the hands of Germany between nine and ten million within their borders and countless millions outside.

When accompanied with the evidence of the destruction of knowledge through book burning and the well-known terrors of world war instigated by the Nazis, it is clear that Germany at the time was a shockingly evil society, hell-bent on destruction. I would also add that Hitler and his minions were *self*-destructive as well as outwardly destructive. It appears that the Chancellor thrived on destruction—destruction in general and of life in particular—and one can rightly assume that if there weren't deformed children, mentally ill adults, Jews, Catholics, or Poles to exterminate, Hitler would have found another group to target for killing. Perhaps Hitler would have gone after people who were too short or those with imperfect vision, or perhaps he would have targeted his hate toward women, or even people who didn't wear his silly style of moustache. It is also reasonable to assume that such a destructive being, when left with nothing to destroy, would ultimately destroy itself.

If self-destruction was their goal (subconscious or otherwise), Hitler and the rest of the Nazis achieved it. Starting with the destruction of knowledge, which turned away great thinkers who eventually worked against the regime, to picking fights that they weren't quite capable of handling (namely, attacking every geographic neighbor and menacing the United States), to killing millions of their own people in the name of healing, the Nazi regime was slowly destroying itself. Hitler, like the coward he most certainly was, eventually self-destructed, too, to the tune of a cyanide capsule and his own pistol.

I don't like to think much about Adolf Hitler, nor do I enjoy dwelling on the horrors of Nazi Germany; but they share a unique place in the collective consciousness—pretty much everyone agrees that they are the epitome of evil in the modern world and a dramatic point can be learned from their example. The people of pre-Nazi Germany, to a large degree, were not abnormal compared to most modern Western cultures. They were perhaps a bit more racist and fairly worse off economically following World War I than what we see now, but, for the most part, they were average Westerners who believed in scientific progress, went to church, and had a healthy pride of country. But, in dramatic fashion, a nation of average Westerners quickly turned into book-burning students, murderous doctors, and warmongers. After all, regular students initiated the book-burning events, everyday physicians administered the euthanasia projects, and normal teenagers went off to fight in the war. To put it bluntly, the disgusting state of affairs that was Nazi Germany could happen anywhere.

Professor Ronald Howard and co-author Clinton Korver make the compelling argument in their book, *Ethics For the Real World*, that we're not far off from where the pre-Nazi Germans were. "It would be comforting to say that we are different, that we wouldn't do such things, that we would hold the line," they argue. "But how do we know?" We do things all the time that compromise what we know to be right moral actions; who's to say that we don't reside on a slippery slope of moral compromise that ends in Nazi-esque killing and self-destruction?

Usually, we rationalize our actions by saying our wrongs are done for a greater good; but the Germans did so as well. The book-burners were "cleansing the literary world," the child-killing doctors were healing, and the genocides were conducted in order to preserve and improve "good heredity," "racial stock," and the general health of the German people—all of which could be seen as a greater good.[68] One good reason the German citizens undertook such evils was their obedience to authority. Under Hitler's Führerprinzip ("leader principle"), everyone in the bureaucratic hierarchy was forced into unquestioning obedience to their superiors, and consequently the suppression of free will. And in Nazi Germany, everyone was involved in the bureaucracy, from political hacks to common physicians.

As we have seen throughout Part VI of *Everyone Agrees*, a substantial population ardently supports self-destructive, evil behavior in many moral debates today, always for some other good. There are those who would create war for reasons besides self-defense, pollute for the sake of production, kill the innocent for a higher standard of living, and trade liberty for some form of security. But if the ideas of concurrence and the contrary examples of the self-destructive Nazis resonate at all, it should be clear that we cannot accept necessary evils, especially when it comes to issues like existence and liberty. We cannot accept preemptive, unnecessary war. We cannot accept degradation of the environment in which we all live. We cannot accept the destruction of human life at any stage. And we cannot accept the deprivation of liberty. We have seen what forces are acting against morality in each of these cases, and we have also seen a clear, logical course to take in each one. We now have a decision to make; we can either be concurrent and use our free will to promote life and liberty for everyone, or we can be contradictory and use our freedom to restrict those same birthrights. I have no doubt that we *can* all take the consistent path and ascend to that metaphorical peak of Mauna Kea. The only question left is will we?

conclusion

I'm a big fan of party tricks. One of my favorites is the wager that someone can't eat five Saltine crackers in a minute or less (it's practically impossible). Then there's the attempt to catch a dollar bill before it drops through one's spaced fingers, and the trick that involves pulling a cork out of a wine bottle after it's been pushed inside. But none of these party tricks are quite as fascinating as the simple question, "What's the most commonly used word in the world?" When I ask people this seemingly easy query, I rarely get the correct answer, even after hours and hours of guesses. As a party trick, the above question is fun. But as a statement about words, ideas, and a universal morality, it's also extremely telling.

It should be easy to figure out what the most commonly used word is—after all, it's spoken all the time. But it's not as easy as you may think. I often hear the good but boring guesses "the" or "a." "The" is certainly the most commonly used word in the *English* language, but, while English is popular, far more people on Earth speak a different language more often. So is it some Chinese word or Hindi term? No, although the Chinese and Indians do use the most commonly used word often. The word in question has transcended language. Is it "hi" or "hello?" Sorry, goodbye. Oh, I know what it is! It's "ciao" or some other trendy European term used all over the world. Again, no. "Yes" or "no?" It must be "no" because "no" is used in both English and Spanish. Nope.

Hopefully, you are dying to find out what this mysterious yet most-used word is. I'll tell you, but not yet. First, I'll give you a clue. The word in question represents the central concept of this book. That is, the word indicates activity in the ah-ha region of the brain; it shows agreement; and it's great for bringing people together. The fact that most people can't guess this word reveals a great deal about us. An idea may be staring us in the face, but we can't see it. It's so obvious yet still obscure—how many people see the concept of concurrence, perhaps.

Like the most commonly used word in the world, concurrence is obvious, though at times obscure to the humans who need to use it for communication and moral decision making. Concurrence is simply the manifestation of logic applied to human communication and morality. When you take a step back, it's obvious that we confuse our perceptions (the information we take in) with our conceptions (our thoughts about that information). It's obvious that disagreements are just miscommunication—either one word applied to two ideas (a dispective) or two words applied to one idea (a monospective). It's also clear that there is a single truth out there. Scientists strive for that truth, and people acknowledge its existence constantly by bickering and arguing (remember, if there wasn't an objective truth, there would be no point in arguing about it). And it's evident that, whatever that objective good is, it must make sense—it must be logical. For something to be morally good, then, it must be good in and of itself.

These truths are all obvious when looked at objectively, but when we're in the heat of an argument or we want to enact vengeance on someone, we lose sight of the fact that communication is imperfect and that our disagreement could be completely artificial. We pit "us" against "them" to feel like we're a part of something and to give more purpose to our lives, yet moral dualism is never fulfilling and always leaves us feeling empty and worn down. And when we are too tired to fight one another, we completely reject the plausibility of right and wrong. In a world where people generally seek their own personal happiness, we lose sight of an objective moral good. Everything becomes morally gray and relativism takes root. Concurrence is obvious, but there are so many things working against it that it becomes obscure.

And so it is with the most commonly used word on Earth. It's used so often, but it's very difficult to come up with at a cocktail party. It's even more difficult to determine where the term came from, as there are hundreds of theories about its origin. The Choctaw Indians and the Burmese have similar-sounding words, and they claim responsibility for the origin. Some attribute the most popular word today to the young Bostonians of the 1800s who enjoyed wordplay and the assignment of acronyms to phrases—"ISBD" for "it shall be done," for example, which is reminiscent of today's use of "IMO" ("in my opinion") or "OMG" ("oh, my God") in text messaging. The kids in Boston came up with a slang version of "all correct" that was spelled "orl korrekt" and then eventually abbreviated to "OK." The Finnish also claim the origin of the number one word; they have a word, "oikea," which means "correct." Latin speakers sometimes use the phrase "Omnis Korecta," sometimes abbreviated as "OK." The British, French, and other groups of Americans all have different claims to the popular term.

Regardless of the origin of the word, "OK," or "okay," took off and is now the most commonly used word on Earth according to many estimates.[1] I can't tell you how many times it was used while I was traveling through a country in which I couldn't speak the native language. The waiter points to a table—"Okay?" The struggling Cantonese speaker responds to a request—"Okay!" The hostel check-in clerk points to the room rate—"Okay?" "Okay."

It's a beautiful word, so easy and universal, and everyone can pronounce it. More importantly, "okay" is used to convey agreement. When you hear "okay," you know you're on the same page, or that you're at least dealing with someone who wants to be on the same page. And "okay" facilitates so many economic transactions, it seems that the tourism industry would go bankrupt if it weren't for that simple little word.

When I hear people using the word "okay," it makes me happy. It means that they are at least trying to communicate and convey ideas, and I know that when we try to do something, we're pretty good at getting it done. So much hardship and waste occurs when we give up and see one group of people as the enemy, or when we lose faith in an objective truth, that it's a pleasure to see people actually come together and agree on something.

We all have the same goals and motivations in life; we all have the same logic that facilitates those motivations; and we all require liberty in order to live full lives. We have so much in common and so much potential. If only we can realize that and be consistent with our thoughts and actions; only then will we be able to take advantage of that potential. A disagreement isn't the end of communication; it's an opportunity to learn. A different label doesn't have to imply opposition; it could just be another way of saying the same thing. And while many people today will scoff at the idea of universal agreement, there is hope. When I tell others the title of this book, pretty much everyone says they *disagree* that everyone can agree. But perhaps that's a start—at least they all agree on that. And perhaps after reading the book, we can all change that rejection of universal agreement at least allow for the possibility of the unifying goal.

When we get past all the confusion that our form of communication presents, it becomes clear that we really do agree. At the core of our agreement is the basis for all truth and moral action: logic itself. If one wants to argue with that idea, he is arguing with the foundations of cognition that allow him to argue in the first place; such is the plight of contradictory morality. Morality is consistent, and it's also self-sufficient. We don't need immorality to act moral; but, conversely, morality is necessary for immorality to exist. In the realm of morality, we don't need it to rain to appreciate the sunshine; moral acts exist without the contrast of immorality. Furthermore, a good end does not justify evil means. Someone can have good intentions, but to act immorally for the sake of the moral leads to a form of morality that justifies basically anything and is contradictory and thus intrinsically wrong.

But what do all these things mean for us in our everyday lives? It may seem impossible to act consistently throughout one's life, but consistency is actually very doable. Besides the well-accepted commandments declared by the Parliament of

212 - conclusion

the World's Religions—don't kill, steal, lie, or commit sexual immorality—concurrence provides guidelines to the big and complex moral dilemmas being debated today. As we saw in the previous part, concurrence provides logical solutions to problems of world conflict, energy, and matters of life—some of the most contentious and seemingly irreconcilable issues today. Most importantly, concurrence gives us a clear direction with regard to human liberty; a free act is only moral if it promotes more free acts. As it is directly related to life and free will, liberty is one of the most important unalienable rights we have, and it is one that everyone can agree on, from believers to atheists, Democrats to Republicans, and everyone in between. If concurrence is the peak of the metaphorical mountain of truth, Mauna Kea, liberty is certainly one of the paths leading to that peak.

Hawaiians have a legend about the real Mauna Kea involving the most beautiful goddess of them all, the snow goddess Poliahu, and the erratic and violent volcano goddess, Pele. In the legend, Poliahu battled Pele for control over the tallest mountain in Hawaii, Mauna Kea. Poliahu brought a blizzard of snow and Pele brought lava flows to the fight. Poliahu had to retreat to the top of Mauna Kea, but she was eventually victorious and banished Pele from the mountain forever.[2]

That is why Mauna Kea is peaceful and dormant and often covered with snow today. Thanks to Poliahu's efforts, we can now ascend Mauna Kea without the threat of Pele's violent volcanic attacks. And, as the natives say, the ascension is well worth the trip. One Hawaiian historian even evokes spiritual terminology when describing it, saying, "Ascending the summit of Mauna Kea takes one closer to the spiritual and the supernatural realm."[3]

Applying the above metaphor to the concepts of concurrence, we can replace Mauna Kea with the mountain of truth, Poliahu with logic, and Pele with the twin obstacles to truth, moral dualism and moral relativism. Using logic to banish moral dualism and moral relativism from the mountain, we are free to ascend to the truth. In doing so, we realize that all our disagreements stem from simple miscommunication; that there really is a universal truth; and that consistency is the root. If you take the trip up Mauna Kea today, you are rewarded with one of the most beautiful—some say the most heavenly—views on Earth. I imagine that the metaphorical peak of Mauna Kea—a universal morality—is one of the most beautiful and heavenly views as well. I hope you agree.

notes

Introduction
1. http://booktv.org/program.aspx?ProgramId=8788&SectionName=&PlayMedia=No. 2. http://www.youtube.com/watch?v=aAwoPLhJVAs. 3. http://www.cnn.com/2008/POLITICS/10/07/presidential.debate.transcript/. 4. Westen 2007:xi. 5. Gardner 2004:92.

The Greatest Peak
6. http://www.soest.hawaii.edu/GG/HCV/maunakea.html. 7. http://www.quotedb.com/quotes/14.

The Game of Life
8. http://www.wired.com/wired/archive/8.12/clinton.html. 9. http://www.quotationspage.com/quote/25384.html.

Coca-Cola, Comedy, and Confusion
1. http://www.snopes.com/cokelore/tadpole.asp. 2. http://www.cs.tut.fi/~jkorpela/wiio.html. 3. http://www.radioopensource.org/hitchens-v-god/.

In the Beginning, There Was the Word
4. Morse 2008a.

Who's Who
5. http://www.baseball-almanac.com/humor4.shtml. 6. http://www.quotedb.com/quotes/704. 7. Beattie 1809. 8. Mobbs et al. 2003. 9. http://www.goodexperience.com/blog/archives/000138.php. 10. Koestler 1990:5. 11. Koestler 1990:230.

Clear As a Bell
12. http://en.wikipedia.org/wiki/Controversies_about_the_word_%22niggardly%22. 13. Bull 2003:112. 14. http://www.slate.com/id/1000162/. 15. http://www.cnn.com/2003/WORLD/meast/05/01/sprj.irq.main/index.html. 16. http://edition.cnn.com/SPECIALS/2003/iraq/forces/casualties/interactive/. 17. http://www.fallacyfiles.org/amphibol.html

Define Your Terms
18. http://www.cnn.com/2008/POLITICS/10/02/debate.transcript/. 19. http://en.wikipedia.org/wiki/Iraq_War_troop_surge_of_2007. 20. http://thinkexist.com/quotation/if_you_wish_to_converse_with_me-define_your/175628.html.

Onward
21. http://scienceworld.wolfram.com/biography/Kelvin.html

Buddhism, Bare Breasts, and Bureaucracy
1. http://omacl.org/Barlaam/parts1-5.html, http://en.wikipedia.org/wiki/Barlaam_and_Josaphat, http://en.wikipedia.org/wiki/Gautama_Buddha, http://home.c2i.net/monsalvat/josaphat.htm.

Believe It or Not
2. http://www.frimmin.com/faith/lotuscross.php. 3. http://www.urbandharma.org/bcdialog/bcd1/buchristdia.html. 4. Johnston 1997:7-8. 5. Newberg, et al 2003, http://www.sciam.com/article.cfm?id=searching-for-god-in-the-brain&page=2. 6. http://www.adherents.com/Religions_By_Adherents.html. 7. http://www.religioustolerance.org/chr_jckr1.htm, http://www.themystica.com/mystica/articles/m/moksa.html, http://www.experiencefestival.com/a/Hinduismvs_Christianity/id/54138. 8. http://www.quotationspage.com/quote/30258.html. 9. De Martino et al. 2006.

Scientific God
10. Persinger 1984. 11. http://www.sciam.com/article.cfm?id=searching-for-god-in-the-brain&page=2. 12. Tolle 2005: 6. 13. The World Almanac and Book of Facts (2008: 711). 14. Hauser 2006:421. 15. Van Biema 2006. 16. http://dictionary.reference.com/browse/agnosticism. 17. http://www.quotationspage.com/quote/4948.html. 18. Persinger 2008 email. 19. Newberg et al. 2003. 20. Francis et al. (1996: 207). 21. http://abcnews.go.com/GMA/Health/Story?id=435412&page=1.

Keeping Abreast on Things
22. http://www.cnn.com/2004/LAW/02/20/findlaw.analysis.hilden.jackson/. 23. Johnston 1898:408. 24. Ellis 1927:1. 25. Féré 2006:48. 26. Ellis 1927:1.

Right, Left, and Down the Drain
27. Luntz (2007: 46). 28. Morse 2008b. 29. http://www.britannica.com/blogs/2007/11/are-you-a-right-wing-or-a-left-wing/. 30. Lewis 2001:xiv. 31. http://www.harrisinteractive.com/harris_poll/index.asp?PID=542. 32. http://www.brainyquote.com/quotes/authors/j/john_kenneth_galbraith.html. 33. Paul (2008:1-3). 34. http://www.quoteland.com/author.asp?AUTHOR_ID=386.

Communication Breakdown
35. Schelling 1960: 55. 36. http://www.nytimes.com/2007/06/23/business/23checkout.html. 37. Morse 2008c. 38. Funder 1987. 39. Funder 1999:75-6. 40. Andreassen 1987. 41. Mulligan 2005. 42. Gladwell 2007. 43. http://www.phrases.org.uk/meanings/305250.html.

Science, Socrates, and Sense
1. Shaw 2004

Relatively Speaking
2. http://www.freudfile.org/psychoanalysis/definition.html. 3. http://faculty.cua.edu/johnsong/hitchcock/pages/psychoanalysis.html. 4. Pentland 1999. 5. De Martino et al. 2006. 6. Ariely quote: Ariely (2008:48).

Weird Science
7. Greene 2005. 8. http://www.time.com/time/magazine/article/0,9171,993016-10,00.html. 9. http://www.lhup.edu/~dsimanek/glossary.htm. 10. http://www.quotationspage.com/quote/9523.html. 11. Greene 2005.

Judgment Day
12. John 8:1.

It Takes Guts
13. http://activatedevolution.blogspot.com/2007/10/heroes-never-black-and-white.html.
14. Katkin et. Al (2001). 15. Bauer et al 1988, Cohen 1996:357. 16. Klein 2004:293.

Everything I Learned I Taught Myself
17. http://www.garlikov.com/Soc_Meth.html

He said, she said
18. http://www.boston.com/yourlife/family/articles/2004/05/27/for_mothers_and_daughters_fightings_part_of_growing_up/. 18. Lewis (2001:4). 19. Koenings et al. 2007. 20. Cameron 1999. 21. Quoted in Heath et al. 2007:164-5.

Misdemeanors, Machiavelli, and Morality
1. http://www.quotedb.com/quotes/3272.

Slap Happy
2. http://en.wikipedia.org/wiki/Sasser_worm. 3. http://news.cnet.com/2100-7349_3-5205107.html. 4. http://www.sophos.com/pressoffice/news/articles/2004/05/va_sasserarrest.html. 5. http://www.wpbf.com/news/16035311/detail.html. 6. http://www.youtube.com/watch?v=Jhs8hHvolM0. 7. http://www.goodreads.com/author/quotes/10994?page=2

The Golden Rule
8. Shermer (2004:19-20). 9. http://law.jrank.org/pages/2482/Alexander-Holmes-Trial-1842.html.

Theory of Concurrence Applied to Morality
10. http://www.departments.bucknell.edu/russian/const/36cons02.html, http://www.answers.com/topic/constitution-of-1936. 11. Pohl 1999. 12. http://en.wikipedia.org/wiki/Politics_of_France. 13. http://en.wikipedia.org/wiki/UN_Security_Council_Resolution_1441. 14. http://home.newadvent.org/cathen/03432a.htm. 15. Kant 2005:100. 16. Kenneth Lay's compensation: http://en.wikipedia.org/wiki/Kenneth_Lay. 17. http://en.wikipedia.org/wiki/Laffer_curve. 18. Lewis 2001:44. 19. Noah and the Whale. "Shape of My Heart." Peaceful, the World Lays Me Down. CherryTree Records, 2008. 20. http://www.philosophypages.com/ph/macv.htm. 21. http://www.philosophypages.com/hy/5i.htm. 22. http://dir.salon.com/story/tech/log/2002/01/15/no_surprises/.

Lincoln's Dilemma
23. http://www.civilwarhome.com/warcosts.htm, http://www.civilwarhome.com/population1860.htm. 24. http://www.geocities.com/timessquare/labyrinth/1164/quote.html. 25. http://www.presidency.ucsb.edu/ws/index.php?pid=29619. 26. http://www.youtube.com/watch?v=jbOE4Ip7In0. 27. http://www.civilwarhome.com/population1860.htm. 28. http://courses.wcupa.edu/jones/his311/notes/plantati.htm, http://www.gongol.com/research/economics/slavebuyout/. 29. Lincoln's objective: http://home.att.net/~rjnorton/Lincoln78.html.

Onward
30. Declaration Toward a Global Ethic 1993. 31. http://www.weltethos.org/dat-english/01-history.htm.

Destruction, DNA, and Deliverance
1. http://www.wired.com/wired/archive/14.01/lying_pr.html. 2. Greene 2001.

Napoleon Dynamite
3. http://en.wikipedia.org/wiki/Napoleon. 4. http://www.historyhome.co.uk/c-eight/france/napfra.htm. 5. http://www.historyhome.co.uk/c-eight/france/napfra.htm. 6. http://www.historyhome.co.uk/c-eight/france/moscow.htm. 7. http://www.adept-plm.com/Newsletter/napoleon.gif. 8. http://en.wikipedia.org/wiki/Napoleon. 9. Morse, Eric Robert 2008:568.

Burn, Baby, Burn
10. Brunekreef 1997, Nevalainen 1998. 11. Friedman 2008:93. 12. http://www.politico.com/news/stories/0908/13179.html. 13. http://www.nytimes.com/2008/08/28/us/politics/28text-obama.html. 14. http://www.msnbc.msn.com/id/27453305. 15. http://www.masshightech.com/stories/2008/08/25/weekly17-Alternative-energy-companies-break-IPO-drought.html. 16. Friedman 2008. 17. http://www.nationmaster.com/graph/eco_gdp-economy-gdp&date=1980. 18. http://en.wikipedia.org/wiki/Energy_Policy_Act_of_2005, http://www.heritage.org/Research/energyandenvironment/bg2020.cfm, http://www.slate.com/id/2169124/. 19. http://www.npr.org/templates/story/story.php?storyId=9647424. 20. http://www.consumeraffairs.com/news04/2006/08/cr_ethanol.html. 21. http://futures.tradingcharts.com/chart/CN/M. 22. http://money.cnn.com/2007/06/19/news/economy/commodity_prices/index.htm, http://www.purdue.edu/uns/x/2008a/080102HurtEthanol.html. 23. http://www.cnn.com/2008/WORLD/americas/04/14/world.food.crisis/. 24. http://en.wikipedia.org/wiki/Hydrogen_production. 25. The World Almanac and Book of Facts 2008:104. 26. http://environment.newscientist.com/article/dn12346-renewable-energy-could-rape-nature.html. 27. http://www.nuc.berkeley.edu/thyd/ne161/ncabreza/sources.html#Safety, http://en.wikipedia.org/wiki/Coal_mining. 28. The World Almanac and Book of Facts 2008:137. 29. The World Almanac and Book of Facts 2008:141.

Life and Death
30. Geri 2008. 31. http://www.cnn.com/US/9810/24/doctor.killed.02/. 32. http://www.boston.com/news/nation/washington/articles/2008/01/17/number_of_abortions_lowest_in_decades/. 33. http://en.wikipedia.org/wiki/Image:UK_abortion_by_gestational_age_2004_histogram.svg. 34. http://www.childdevelopmentinfo.com/development/prenataldevelopment.shtml, http://www.britannica.com/EBchecked/topic/409709/human-nervous-system/261745/Prenatal-and-postnatal-development-of-the-human-nervous-system. 35. http://www.ornl.gov/sci/techresources/Human_Genome/home.shtml. 36. http://www.rainbowkids.com/ArticleDetails.aspx?id=618. 37. http://www.deathpenaltyinfo.org/costs-death-penalty. 38. http://www.deathpenaltyinfo.org/innocence-list-those-freed-death-row.

Let Freedom Reign
39. http://historymatters.gmu.edu/d/5057/. 40. http://www.whitehouse.gov/news/releases/2008/09/20080924-10.html. 41. http://ipsnews.net/news.asp?idnews=44168. 42. http://www.whitehouse.gov/news/releases/2008/09/20080924-10.html. 43. http://www.wbur.org/news/2008/80534_20081007.asp. 44. http://articles.latimes.com/2008/jul/16/nation/na-losingfaith16. 45. http://www.iep.utm.edu/f/freewill.htm. 46. http://www.quotationspage.com/quote/29913.html. 47. Stotland & Blumenthal 1964, Langer 1975. 48. http://www.usatoday.com/news/health/2007-08-25-happiness_N.htm. 49. Rodin

et al. 1977. 50. https://www.cia.gov/library/publications/the-world-factbook/rankorder/2102rank.html, Freedom House 2008. 51. The Heritage Foundation 2008. 52. http://www.ushistory.org/Declaration/document/index.htm. 53. http://en.wikipedia.org/wiki/Federal_Register. 54. http://www.whitehouse.gov/news/releases/2008/09/20080924-10.html. 55. http://realserver.bu.edu:8080/ramgen/w/b/wbur/storage/2008/10/morningedition_1007_2.rm. 56. http://query.nytimes.com/gst/fullpage.html?res=9C0DE7DB153EF933A0575AC0A96F958260&sec=&spon=&partner=permalink&exprod=permalink. 57. http://www.fundinguniverse.com/company-histories/Fannie-Mae-Company-History.html, http://hnn.us/articles/1849.html, http://en.wikipedia.org/wiki/Fannie_mae. 58. http://www.washingtonpost.com/wp-dyn/content/article/2008/06/09/AR2008060902626.html. 59. http://query.nytimes.com/gst/fullpage.html?res=9C0DE7DB153EF933A0575AC0A96F958260&sec=&spon=&partner=permalink&exprod=permalink. 60. http://en.wikipedia.org/wiki/The_Testament_of_Freedom. 61. http://thinkexist.com/quotations/liberty/.

Onward

62. http://en.wikipedia.org/wiki/Nazi_book_burnings. 63. Stars. "Your Ex-Lover Is Dead Set Yourself on Fire. Arts and Crafts, 2005. 64. Lifton 2000:50-1. 65. Lifton 2000:56. 66. http://en.wikipedia.org/wiki/Action_T4. 67. http://www.historyplace.com/worldwar2/holocaust/h-euthanasia.htm. 68. Reasons: Lifton 2000:42.

Conclusion

1. Bragg 2004. 2. http://hawaii.aloha-hawaii.com/hawaii/mauna+kea/. 3. http://www.malamamaunakea.org/hawaiianculture.php?article_id=16.

bibliography

Aitken, Robert, and David Steindl-Rast. The Ground We Share: Everyday Practice, Buddhist and Christian. Boston: Shambhala, 1996.

Andersson, Bjorn, and Christina Karrqvist. "How Swedish pupils, aged 12-15 years, understand light and its properties." International Journal of Science Education, 5 (1983): 387-402.

Andreassen, Paul B. "On the social psychology of the stock market: Aggregate attributional effects and the regressiveness of prediction." Journal of Personality and Social Psychology 53 (1987): 490+.

Ariely, Dan. Predictably Irrational: The Hidden Forces That Shape Our Decisions. New York: HarperCollins, 2008.

Ashley, Aaron D. Review of Data of Jewish Americans. Rep. U.S. Department of Defense, Defense Equal Opportunity Management Institute. 2000.

Bauer, R. M., and M. Verfaellie. "Electrodermal discrimination of familiar but not unfamiliar faces in prosopagnosia." Brain Cognition 8 (1988): 240-52.

Beattie, James. Essays: on the Nature and Immutability of Truth, in Opposition to Sophistry and Scepticism. Philadelphia: Hopkins & Earle, 1809. Google Books. 17 Apr. 2008<http://books.google.com/books?id=MFsBAAAAYAAJ>.

Brafman, Ori, and Rom Brafman. Sway: The Irresistible Pull of Irrational Behavior. New York: Broadway Books, 2008.

Bragg, Melvyn. The Adventure of English : The Biography of a Language. New York: Arcade Publishing, 2004.
Brunekreef, B. "Air pollution and life expectancy: is there a relation?" Occupational and Environmental Medicine 54 (1997): 781-84.
Bull, Peter. The Microanalysis of Political Communication: Claptrap and Ambiguity. New York: Routledge, 2003.
Cameron, Lisa A. "Raising the Stakes in the Ultimatum Game: Experimental Evidence from Indonesia." Economic Inquiry 37 (1999): 47-59.
CIA. "Life Expectancy at Birth." CIA Factbook. CIA. 16 Sept. 2008 <https://www.cia.gov/library/publications/the-world-factbook/rankorder/2102rank.html>.
Cohen, Jonathan D., and Jonathan W. Schooler, eds. Scientific Approaches to Consciousness. Mahwah, NJ: Lawrence Erlbaum Associates, Inc., 1996.
De Martino, Benedetto, Dharshan Kumaran, Ben Seymour, and Raymond J. Dolan. "Frames, Biases, and Rational Decision-Making in the Human Brain." Science 313 (2006): 684-87.
De Mey, Tim. "Tales of the Unexpected: Incongruity-Resolution in Humor Comprehension, Scientific Discovery, and Thought Experimentation." Logic and Logical Philosophy 14 (2005): 69-88.
Dixit, Jay. "Wisecrackers." Psychology Today Sept.-Oct. 2008: 84-89.
"Global Ethic Foundation | Text of the Declaration.". <http://www.weltethos.org/dat-english/03-declaration.htm>. 4 Sept. 1993. Parliament of the World's Religions. 23 Sept. 2008 <http://www.weltethos.org>.
Ellis, Havelock. Studies in the Psychology of Sex, Vol. 1. Ottawa: EbooksLib, 1927.
Ellison, Christopher G. "Are Religious People Nice People? Evidence from the National Survey of Black Americans." Social Forces 71 (1992).
Fere, Charles. The Evolution and Dissolution of the Sexual Instinct. Whitefish, MT: Kessinger Publishing, 2006.
Francis, Leslie J., William K. Kay, and William S. Campbell, eds. Research in Religious Education. London: Gracewing, Limited, 1996.
Freedom House. "Tables and Charts." Freedom House. 16 Sept. 2008 <http://www.freedomhouse.org/template.cfm?page=25&year=2008>.
Friedman, Thomas L. Hot, Flat, and Crowded: Why We Need a Green Revolution—and How It Can Renew America. New York: Farrar, Straus & Giroux, 2008.
Funder, David C., and C. R. Colvin. "Friends and strangers: acquaintanceship, agreement, and the accuracy of personality judgment." Journal of Personality and Social Psychology 55 (1988): 149-58.
Funder, David C., and Kathryn M. Dobroth. "Differences between traits: Properties associated with interjudge agreement." Journal of Personality and Social Psychology 52 (1987): 409-18.
Funder, David C. Personality Judgment: A Realistic Approach to Person Perception. New York: Academic Press, 1999.
"Game Theory." Wikipedia. 30 June 2008 <http://en.wikipedia.org/wiki/Game_theory>.
Gardner, Howard. Changing Minds: The Art and Science of Changing Our Own and Other People's Minds. New York: Harvard Business School Press, 2004.
Geri. "Reaction of Sidewalk Counseling at Abortion Clinics." E-mail interview. 3 Dec. 2008.
Gladwell, Malcolm. Blink: The Power of Thinking Without Thinking. New York: Back Bay Books, 2007.
Greene, Brian. The Fabric of the Cosmos: Space, Time, and the Texture of Reality. New York: Vintage, 2005.

Greene, Joshua D., R. Brian Sommerville, Leigh E. Nystrom, John M. Darley, and Jonathan D. Cohen. "An fMRI Investigation of Emotional Engagement in Moral Judgment." Science 293 (2001): 2105-108.

Haidt, Jonathan. "The Emotional Dog and its Rational Tail: A Social Intuitionist Approach to Moral Judgment." Psychological Review 108 (2001): 814-34.

Haist, Frank, Allen W. Song, Krista Wild, Tracy L. Faber, Carol A. Popp, and Robin D. Morris. "Linking Sight and Sound: fMRI Evidence of Primary Auditory Cortex Activation during Visual Word Recognition." Brain and Language 76:3 (2001): 340-55. Science Direct.

Hauser, Marc. Moral Minds: How Nature Designed Our Universal Sense of Right and Wrong. New York: Ecco Press, 2006.

Heath, Chip, and Dan Heath. Made to Stick: Why Some Ideas Survive and Others Die. New York: Random House, 2007.

The Heritage Foundation. "Index of Economic Freedom." The Heritage Foundation. 16 Sept. 2008 <http://www.heritage.org/Index/countries.cfm>.

Howard, Ronald A., and Clinton Korver. Ethics for the Real World: Creating a Personal Code to Guide Decisions in Work and Life. New York: Harvard Business School Press, 2008.

John 8:1.

Johnston, Harry Hamilton. British Central Africa: An Attempt to Give Some Account of a Portion of the Territories Under British Influence North of the Zambesi . London: Metheun & Co., 1897.

Johnston, William. Christian Zen: A Way of Meditation. New York: Fordham University Press, 1997.

Joyce, C. Alan, ed. The World Almanac and Book of Facts 2008. New York: World Almanac Books, 2007.

Kane, Robert, ed. The Oxford Handbook of Free Will. New York: Oxford University Press, 2004.

Kant, Immanuel. Critique of Pure Reason. Forgotten Books, 2008.

Kant, Immanuel. The Moral Law: Groundwork of the Metaphysic of Morals. New York: Routledge, 2005.

Katkin, Edward S., Stefan Wiens, and Anne Ohman. "Nonconscious Fear Conditioning, Visceral Perception, and the Development of Gut Feelings." Psychological Science 12 (2001): 366-70. PubMed.

Klein, Gary. The Power of Intuition: How to Use Your Gut Feelings to Make Better Decisions at Work. New York: Broadway Books, 2004.

Koenigs, Michael, and Daniel Tranel. "Irrational Economic Decision-Making after Ventromedial Prefrontal Damage: Evidence from the Ultimatum Game." The Journal of Neuroscience 27 (2007): 951-56.

Koestler, Arthur. The Act of Creation. New York: Penguin (Non-Classics), 1990.

Kuhn, Thomas S. The Copernican Revolution: Planetary Astronomy in the Development of Western Thought. Cambridge: Harvard University Press, 1985.

Langer, Ellen J., et al. "Reduction of Psychological Stress in Surgical Patients." Journal of Experimental Social Psychology 11 (1975): 155-65.

Lewis, C. S. Mere Christianity. San Francisco: HarperCollins, 2001.

Lifton, Robert J. The Nazi Doctors: Medical Killing and the Psychology of Genocide. New York: Basic Books, 2000.

Luntz, Frank. Words that Work: It's Not what You Say, It's what People Hear. New York: Hyperion, 2007.

McCusker, Rachel R., et al. "Caffeine Content of Decaffeinated Coffee." Journal of Analytical Toxicology 30 (2006): 611-13. Mobbs, Dean, Michael D. Greicius, Eiman Abdel-Azim, Vinod Menon, and Allan L. Reiss. "Humor Modulates the Mesolimbic Reward Centers." Neuron 40 (2003): 1041-048.

Morse, Eric Robert. Monaco. San Diego: New Classic Books, 2008.

Morse, Joseph. Define "God" Vers. Unpublished study, Amelior Institute.

Morse, Joseph. Defining Political Wing Poll Results. Unpublished study, Amelior Institute. 2008.

Morse, Joseph. Imagine a Sports Car Poll Results. Unpublished study, Amelior Institute. 2008.

Mulligan, Elizabeth J., and Reid Hastie. "Explanations determine the impact of information on financial investment judgments." Journal of Behavioral Decision Making 18 (2005): 145-56.

Nevalainen, Jaakko, and Juha Pekkanen. "The effect of particulate air pollution on life expectancy." The Science of the Total Environment 217 (1998): 137-41.

Newberg, Andrew, Michael Pourdehnad, Abass Alavi, and Eugene G. D'Aquili. "Cerebral Blood Flow During Meditative Prayer: Preliminary Findings and Methodological Issues." Perceptual and Motor Skills 97 (2003): 625-30. American Psychological Association.

Paul, Ron. The Revolution: A Manifesto. New York: Grand Central Publishing, 2008.

PBS, prod. "Make Up Your Mind." Scientific American Frontiers. PBS. 15 Oct. 2002.

Pentland, Alex, and Andrew Liu. "Modeling and Prediction of Human Behavior." Neural Computation 11 (1999): 229-42.

Persinger, M.A. "People who report religious experiences may also display enhanced temporal lobe signs." Perceptual and Motor Skills. 58 (1984): 963-75. PubMed.

Pohl, J. Otto. Ethnic Cleansing in the USSR, 1937-1949. New York: Greenwood Publishing Group, 1999.

"Relativity Explained!" Anecdotage.com. 30 June 2008 <http://www.anecdotage.com/index.php?aid=14050>.

Rodin, Judith, and Ellen J. Langer. "Long-Term Effects of a Control-Relevant Intervention With the Institutionalized Ages." Journal of Personality and Social Psychology 35 (1977): 897-902.

Schelling, Thomas C. "The Strategy of Conflict: Prospectus for a Reorientation of Game Theory." The Journal of Conflict Resolution 2 (1958): 203-64. 12 May 2008 <http://www.jstor.org/pss/172793>.

Shakespeare, William, William Allan Neilson, and W. J. Craig. The Complete Works of William Shakespeare. Cambridge: Houghton Mifflin, 1906. Google Books. 5 July 2008 <http://books.google.com/books?id=HjBNCENW2ycC&pg=PR1&client=firefox-a&source=gbs_selected_pages&cad=0_0#PPR3,M1>.

Shaw, Bernard, and Imogen Stubbs. Saint Joan: A Chronicle Play in Six Scenes and an Epilogue. Ed. Dan H. Laurence. New York: Penguin Classics, 2001.

Shermer, Michael. The Science of Good and Evil: Why People Cheat, Gossip, Care, Share, and Follow the Golden Rule. New York: Macmillan, 2005.

Stanford University. "Game Theory." Stanford Encyclopedia of Philosophy. 25 Jan. 1997. Stanford University. 6 Dec. 2008 <http://plato.stanford.edu/entries/game-theory/>.

Stars. Your Ex-Lover Is Dead. Rec. 8 Mar. 2005. MP3. 2005.

Stotland, E., and Al Blumenthal. "The Reduction of Anxiety a a Result of the Expectation of Making a Choice." Canadian Journal of Psychology 18 (1964): 139-45.

Taleb, Nassim Nicholas. Fooled by Randomness : The Hidden Role of Chance in Life

    <u>and in the Markets</u>. New York: Random House, 2008.
Tolle, Eckhart. <u>A New Earth: Awakening to Your Life's Purpose</u>. New York: Dutton Adult, 2005.
Van Biema, David. "God vs. Science." <u>Time</u> 13 Nov. 2006: 48-55.
Westen, Drew. <u>The Political Brain: The Role of Emotion in Deciding the Fate of the Nation</u>. New York: PublicAffairs, 2007.
<u>The World Almanac and Book of Facts</u>. New York: World Almanac Books, 2007.

Printed in the United States
209679BV00002B/1-105/P